4

Ingredients

Ingredients

4 Ingredients
PO Box 1171
Mooloolaba QLD 4557

ABN 19 307 118 068

BN20046832

www.4ingredients.com.au
info@4ingredients.com.au

Published by 4 Ingredients 2007
First printed March 2007
Reprinted twice in April 2007
Reprinted May 2007
Reprinted June 2007
Reprinted July 2007
Reprinted August 2007
Reprinted September 2007
Reprinted October 2007

Design : Nigel Forbes
Typesetting : BlueCrystal Creative ; www.bluecrystalcreative.com
Printed and bound in Singapore

ISBN 978-0-646-47080-1

Foreword

Food is the cheapest form of entertainment. When I was traveling and backpacking around Europe in my late teens I couldn't afford to do too much except enjoy the countryside, walk through the city streets and hike the beautiful mountains. But what I could afford to do was enjoy food and conversation with a group of friends.

The fact that this recipe book is made up of recipes with just **4 ingredients** makes it a very easy, cheap way to have fun. Food surrounds everything we do; from the minute we wake up till we go to bed we punctuate our life around our meals and snacks. So why not make it easy and healthy at the same time with this refreshing, extraordinary recipe book.

When I want to, or have to make a meal, I often spend some time looking for a recipe, the reason being as many recipes which have lots of ingredients I usually find I am missing one or more ingredients, so I have to keep looking until I find a recipe with all the ingredients. With this recipe book you will always have the ingredients; the guide of what you should stock your pantry with will help.

If you are going to make the effort to make food, why not make it healthy! Most foods whether it is chocolate cake, lemon butter or custard can be healthy, it all depends on the ingredients you use. So buy good quality ingredients and all the recipes in this book will be healthy. But what is good quality? What is healthy? The media and science has confused the masses, most of us throw up our hands in despair and decide to just eat what we want. So I'm going to make it easy. "Nature makes all the healthy foods and everything else is junk".

Ask yourself the following; who makes margarine, artificial sweeteners, additives, modified milks and the like? So when you are choosing the ingredients for your recipes make sure they are the best, choose butter, organic eggs, organic unbleached flour, rapadura sugar (instead of white sugar), real mayonnaise, pastry made with butter, cold pressed oils fresh fruit and vegetables and the like.

The rule is 80/20, for 80% of the time eat good wholesome foods, but remember to have fun and enjoy the other side as well, but just 20%.

Congratulations Rachael and Kim, what a fabulous book for busy Mums and Dads as well as a great book for all ages, from the teenage years to the older generation. Everyone will reap the benefits of this fabulous **4 ingredients** cookbook.

Cyndi O'Meara

Nutritionist, Presenter and Author of Changing Habits Changing Lives.

Introduction

Have you ever experienced any of the following?

1. *You look at your watch at you think 'Gosh, it's 5:00 O'clock" what am I going to cook for dinner?*
2. *You collect your child from school and immediately they ask, "What's for dinner?"*
3. *You are DEFINITELY leaving work at 5:01pm and are still at your desk at 6:30pm...*
4. *You spend hours on the phone trying to explain how to cook something to your child who has just moved out?*
5. *OH MY GOD...They're coming for dinner!!!*
6. *Soccer practice goes longer than anticipated and you are just starting dinner at 6:00...*
7. *Go to the pantry look at it (full to the brim) and think "Nothing in there!"*
8. *Find yourself cooking spaghetti bolognaise for the kids AGAIN!!!*
9. *Spend all afternoon cooking and then have to clean what feels like a million things.*
10. *Have a hot date and want to impress and don't know where to start?*
11. *Groan and stress at the very thought of having to shop for 400 ingredients not to mention the big hole in the wallet afterwards?*
12. *Feel excited about cooking great food but without breaking the weekly food budget?*

And many other challenging culinary crises?

WELL THIS BOOK IS FOR YOU!

And your family, your friends
and their family and their friends....

The whole concept of 4 Ingredients is to make preparing quick, easy and delicious food by;

Reducing the number of ingredients required to make something yummy. Every one of these fabulous recipes are made with only four or less ingredients. Our aim was to simplify without compromising on flavour, and just to be sure, we have tried and tested every recipe in this book!

Reduce the number of utensils required to make something yummy. The only measuring utensils required to make the recipes in this book are 1 teaspoon, 1 tablespoon and 1 cup. Remaining measurements eg., millilitre (ml) or grams (g) can be purchased off the shelf in those quantities.

Reduce the amount of money spent on food each week. Food is one of the largest items in the weekly budget so it is well worth shopping around for good quality food at a reasonable price. By reducing the ingredients, you do not need to buy as much. A recipe with 8 ingredients generally costs more to prepare than a recipe with 4.

Create more time to spend doing what you love to do. By simplifying the recipe you often simplify the clean up this equates to saved time ... Something most could do with more of these days.

We are two ordinary Mums who absolutely love and adore our families. We are both career Mums still actively working within our professions, but we work our schedules around our gorgeous children and families and like most busy Mums are always appreciative of ways to create more time for them.

The reality of 4 Ingredients began when Rachael presented Kim with a signed copy of her new book "Read My Lips!" Kim was admiring what her extremely talented friend had achieved when Rachael remarked "everyone has a good book inside them!" And a little while later the very courageous and creative Mrs McCosker validated that statement by casually mentioning her own book idea to Rachael "What is it?" Rach asked, 'A book full of yummy recipes with 4 or fewer ingredients'....

"BRILLIANT!" Rachael exclaims, "You HAVE to do it!"

"Too hard, no time" Kim replies

"No way" says the unstoppable Mrs Bermingham

"Love…I've had this idea for years, I've been collecting recipes for years and have never done anything with it. I'll sit on it for years more because the mere thought of writing a book is SCARIER than a teething toddler … AND THEY ARE SCARY … (We both currently have them)!!!"

"It's not that hard" Rach says

And Kim replied "Yeah …you write it with me then!!!!"

And the rest as they say is history…

We have spent hours upon hours upon hours gathering the recipes for 4 Ingredients from our nearest and dearest. We have spent further hours upon hours upon hours preparing these recipes with our nearest and dearest. To each of you, way too many to list individually, THANK-YOU. Thank you for your input, your advice, your wisdom and the laughs.

We have had a sensational time putting this book together, and are positive the recipes that we've had such delight in preparing and devouring will also consume your kitchens with love and laughs, and satisfy and fill many an empty belly.

But whatever happens the greatest reward we have already received … A strengthened friendship between two great friends who have known each other since kindergarten.

Personal thanks from Kim…

My sincerest thanks go to you Rach, you are an inspiration, an amazing woman and I am blessed to have you in my life … This is real because of you!!

To the ABSOLUTE Loves of my life. My husband Glen, how did I ever cope prior to you? And my two BEAUTIFUL boys Morgan and Hamilton – you three have bought more happiness and love into my life than should be legal. All I do, I do for you (except those little shopping excursions every now and then when true, true - it's all about me!!).

Personal thanks from Rachael…

Kim McCosker (Turnbull) I am so privileged and so very thankful that you entrusted your dream with me and am thrilled that I was able to help you bring it into a reality. Not only are you one of the most dynamic, passionate, energetic, generous and efficient women I know – you are an outstanding mother, business woman and friend and an extraordinary role model for all around you. Not many people could write a book within 5 months but with your remarkable drive and enthusiasm it has been incredibly easy and LOTS of fun! Thank you for instigating it! Thanks to my wonderful husband Paul for his eagerness in taste testing and our gorgeous son Jaxson who kept me entertained with his numerous medley of musicals on my pots and pans. To my Darling brother 'Spud' a very talented Chef whose guidance in con-structing this book has been invaluable.

And finally from us both…

To anyone out there who has ever thought, "What am I going to cook for dinner?" This book is for you and your family and your friends and their family and their friends …

In The Cupboard

4 Ingredients offers a wide range of yummy recipes, cooked for our families and friends for many a BBQ, party, Sunday dinner, Friday drinks and so on. In all our trials and errors there seemed to be a bunch of staple ingredients we always called upon. What we aim to do in this section is help you stock your kitchen pantry with those basic ingredients that will help flavour, make and save many a dish and event from peril.

Please note: In this book we have not included salt, pepper & water as part of the 4 Ingredients.

Savoury

Sea salt
Peppercorns
Vinegar
Lemons
Soy sauce
Fresh garlic
Sesame oil & seeds
Minced ginger
Sweet-chilli sauce
Whole-egg mayonnaise
Garlic
Basil Pesto
Cold pressed extra
virgin macadamia oil
Extra virgin macadamia
oil spray
Bread crumbs
Sour cream
Tinned soups; mushroom,
chicken, tomato, asparagus,
French onion soup
Dijon mustard

Sweet

Plain flour
Self-raising flour
Rapadura sugar
Icing sugar
Food colouring
Vanilla essence
Condensed milk
Cream cheese
Puff pastry
Mixed fruit
Jams; apricot, strawberry
Arrowroot biscuits
Honey

Caster sugar

Evaporated milk
Mixed spices

Cinnamon
(dry mix) Nutmeg
Cornflour

Wholegrain mustard
Spaghetti & Noodles
Brown rice
Jasmine rice
Sesame seeds
Pine nuts
Tomato sauce
BBQ sauce
Worcestershire sauce
Beef and chicken stock cubes
Curry powder

Eggs
Marmalade
Gelatine
Tin of crushed pineapple
Jelly crystals
Packet of bamboo skewers

Guide to weights and measures

A big fancy conversion table is not required, as all you need to make the recipes within 4 Ingredients are:

1 Teaspoon
1 Tablespoon
1 Cup
... *and a pinch of love!!*

Abbreviations used

Gram   g
Kilogram   kg
Millilitre ml

Oven temperature guide

Making friends with your oven really helps when cooking. Basically the Celsius temperature is about half the Fahrenheit temperature.

A lot of ovens these days offer the option to bake or fan bake (amongst others), as a rule, having the fan assisted option on will greatly increase the temperature in your oven and will shorten cooking times.

Our recipes have been compiled assuming a static conventional oven (non fan-forced) unless otherwise stated. If however your oven is fan forced as a general rule of thumb, conventional cooking temperatures are reduced by 20C (this may vary between models). So if the recipe reads bake for 1 hour at 200C that will be 1 hour at 180C fan-forced.

Here's some help:

	Fahrenheit	Celsius	Gas Mark
Slow	275	140	1
Slow	300	150	2
Mod	325	165	3
Mod	350	180	4
Mod hot	375	190	5
Mod hot	400	200	6
Hot	425	220	7
Hot	450	230	8
Very hot	475	240	9

Healthy Food Substitutes

What we would really have loved is to have substituted many of our everyday household products for healthier alternatives. The main reason being is that natural, non-technically enhanced products are LOADED with essential nutrients that fuel your body, mind and soul. Apart form the obvious short and long term benefits of consuming these ingredients, you can literally taste the difference.

However not wanting to isolate those that are not able to purchase these products readily, we did not include these within our recipes, opting instead to add this section, which we feel, is vital to your and your families' health. For those of you able to access these products readily the table below will show you what mainstream ingredient can be easily substituted with a healthier (and less technically altered and therefore nutrient drained) alternative. For more information on this we recommend our good friend Cyndi O'Meara's book Changing Habits Changing Lives:

Product	Substitute
Sugar	• Rapadura Sugar / Organic Raw Sugar*
Oil	• Cold pressed Extra Virgin Olive Oil*
	• Cold Pressed Macadamia Nut Oil*
Spray Oil	• Cold Pressed Macadamia Nut Oil *
Flour	• Spelt Flour
	• Organic Plain Flour and Organic
Baking Powder	• Organic Self Raising Flour*
Margarine	• Butter
Eggs	• Organic Free Range Eggs*
Milk	• Organic Milk*
	• Raw Milk
Pasta	• Made from fresh ingredients
	• Organic Pasta*
Honey	• Manuka Honey*
	• Organic Honey*
Jams	• Organic Jam*
	• Homemade Jams made from raw ingredients
Soy Sauce	• Tamari Soy Sauce*

Note – all ingredients with an asterisk * can now be bought in your local supermarket.

Table Of Contents

Breakfasts

Eat breakfast like a king, lunch like a prince and dinner like a pauper

Adelle Davis

Bacon & Egg Muffin

Makes 1. A recipe from Brett McCosker.

- *1 English muffin*
- *1 egg*
- *1 rasher of bacon*
- *1 tbs. BBQ Sauce*

Fry your egg and bacon, place on absorbent paper. Toast muffin in a toaster, spread with BBQ sauce and top with bacon and egg.

Optional: Add a slice of cheese.

Bircher Muesli

Serves 1

- *½ cup natural muesli*
- *¼ cup orange juice mixed with*
- *2 tbs. low-fat natural yoghurt and*
- *1 green apple, grated*

Soak the muesli in the juice for 15 minutes. Mix in remaining ingredients and serve!!

Citrus Pancakes

Makes 4. Our children love these.

- *1 cup self raising flour*
- *1 egg*
- *1 cup milk*
- *1 orange – finely grate the peel from the whole orange*

Sift flour; add egg and a pinch of salt. Beat gradually adding milk until thick and smooth. Add orange zest. Heat non-stick frying pan. Pour desired quantity into frying pan, cook until bubbling on top and then flip.

Optional: Serve with maple syrup, lemon juice and sugar, honey or stewed fruits.

Crumpets with Strawberries

Serves 2

- *4 crumpets*
- *2 tbs. honey*
- *8 strawberries washed, hulled and sliced*
- *200g tub mocha flavoured yoghurt*

Toast crumpets. Drizzle the crumpets evenly with honey. Top with strawberries and yoghurt.

Damper

Serves 2. Thanks for the idea, Jeremy Horwood.

- *2 cups self raising flour*
- *1.5 cups milk*
- *1 tsp. sugar*
- *1 tsp. butter*

Sift the flour and sugar into a bowl and add a pinch of salt. Add butter and enough milk (1 cup) to make a manageable dough. Shape into a flat ball and place on a greased and floured oven tray, bake at 220C for 25-30 minutes baste with milk during cooking.

Optional: Serve hot with lashings of butter and golden syrup or jam.

English Muffin with Strawberries

Serves 1. This is a really lovely way to start the day!

- *1 English muffin*
- *2 tsp. low fat cream cheese*
- *6 fresh strawberries, washed, hulled and quartered*
- *2 tbs. maple syrup*

Cut muffin in half and toast. Spread cream cheese on both muffins, top with strawberries and drizzle with maple syrup.

Fluffy Cheese Omelette

Makes 2

- *3 eggs*
- *½ cup cheese, finely grated*
- *1 tbs. butter*

Beat whites of eggs stiffly with pinch of salt. Lightly fold in yolks and 3 tbs. cold water, then grated cheese. Melt butter in a pan and when very hot pour in mixture. Cook till golden brown underneath. Brown top under griller, or turn with egg flipper.

Grilled Apple, Banana & Ricotta Stack

Makes 1. This is a charming breakfast; your guests will be impressed!

- *1 apple*
- *1 banana*
- *2 tbs. reduced fat fresh ricotta*
- *1 tbs. honey*

Slice and grill the apple for 3 minutes. Layer apple and banana. Top with ricotta and drizzle honey over all.

Optional: This is also delicious done with pear rather than apple, or a combination of both.

Grilled Grapefruit

Makes 2

- 2 medium grapefruit (ruby-red and rio-red are sweeter varieties)
- 1 tbs. honey
- 1 tbs. brown sugar
- 200g tub lite vanilla yoghurt

Halve grapefruits and carefully loosen pulp with a sharp knife. Combine honey and brown sugar. Place grapefruit in a small oven-proof dish and drizzle with the honey/sugar mixture. Place under preheated grill for 3-4 minutes, or until slightly browned. Serve with yoghurt.

Grilled Pears with Yoghurt

Makes 2

- 2 pears
- 4 tbs. yoghurt (flavour of your choice)

Slice and grill pears for 3 minutes. Top with yoghurt.

Healthy Breakfast on the go

Serves 4

- 1 tub fruil yoghurt
- 1 organic free-range egg
- 2 cups diced watermelon
- 2 cups other diced fruit (banana, strawberries, pineapple, apples)

Place all ingredients into a blender and serve. A fantastic breakfast to take with you.

Praline Toast

Serves 4

- *6 slices bread*
- *¼ cup butter, softened*
- *¼ cup pecans, finely chopped*
- *½ cup brown sugar*

Mix together butter, pecans and sugar then spread it on bread slices. Place in preheated 180C oven and bake until brown and bubbly.

Waffles

Serves 4

- *2 cups self-raising flour*
- *½ cup oil*
- *½ cup milk*

Preheat waffle iron. Combine all ingredients in a bowl and mix well, pour ¾ cup of batter into the waffle iron and cook until golden brown.

Waffle, Strawberries & Yoghurt

Serves 4

- *8 waffles*
- *1 punnet strawberries, washed, hulled and quartered*
- *200g tub vanilla yoghurt*

Lightly toast the waffles. Fold half the strawberries through the yoghurt and pour over the waffles. Top with remaining strawberries.

Zucchini Fritters

Serves 2

- *2 eggs*
- *¼ red onion, grated*
- *½ zucchini, grated*
- *2 tbs. carrot, grated*

Beat eggs and add remaining ingredients, season for taste. Heat a small non-stick frying pan over medium heat. Spoon 2 x 2 tbs. of mixture into the pan, leaving room for spreading.
Cook for 2 minutes each side.

Dips, Salad Dressings & Sauces

There is more hunger for love and appreciation in this world than for bread.

Mother Teresa

Avocado Salsa

A recipe from Michelle Dodd.

- *1 large ripe avocado*
- *½ vine ripened tomato*
- *½ red onion*
- *3 tbs. coriander, chopped*

Dice avocado, reserving seed, tomato and onion, add coriander and mix well. Place the seed back into the dip to help prevent discolouration and refrigerate until needed.

Optional: Add a splash of extra virgin olive oil

Corn Relish Dip

- *1 cup cream cheese*
- *1 small jar of corn relish*

Beat cheese until smooth, add corn relish.

Crab Dip

Recipe from Cyndi O'Meara.

- *1 cup cream cheese, softened*
- *¾ cup sweet chilli sauce*
- *1 cup crabmeat*

Spread cream cheese on a small platter, cover with chilli sauce and sprinkle with crabmeat.

French Onion Dip

- *1 cup sour cream*
- *1/3 packet French onion soup*

Mix soup into sour cream and chill.

Garlic Avocado Dip

- *2 large ripe avocados*
- *2 large cloves fresh garlic*
- *1 tsp. sea salt*
- *1 lemon*

Peel and de-seed avocado, reserving seed. Place salt and garlic into a mortar and pound until well combined. Place avocado and garlic salt mix into a food processor together with the juice of ½ a lemon. Blend well and check seasoning. Place the seed back into the dip to help prevent discolouration and refrigerate until needed.

Grilled Cheese Salsa Dip

A Mexicana marvel ... too easy and too tasty!

- *250g edam or gouda*
- *2 tbs. cream*
- *½ cup salsa*

Shred cheese, place in small saucepan. Cook on low-medium stovetop; let cheese melt then add cream, stirring frequently to make sure cheese doesn't scorch the dish. Transfer to a warm dish, top with salsa.

Optional: Serve with fresh raw vegetables and corn chips ... mmmm-mmm!

Holy Guacamole

A recipe from the very bright Yvonne Ormsby.

- *3 avocados*
- *¼ cup sour cream*
- *½ cup salsa*
- *Corn chips*

Mash avocados, add salsa, sour cream and a pinch of sea salt and mix well. Serve with corn chips.

Hummus

A recipe by Michelle Dodd.

- *300g can chickpeas*
- *1 garlic clove crushed*
- *2 tbs. lemon juice*
- *1 tbs. tahini*

Blend all ingredients in a food processor.

Optional: Serve with julienne vegetables and crackers.

Ricotta & Chutney Dip

- *1 cup ricotta cheese*
- *½ cup of mango chutney (any fruit chutney is nice)*
- *¼ cup mixed nuts chopped*
- *1 pkt poppadums*

Mix ricotta and chutney until well combined, then add nuts. Serve with poppadums.

Smoked Salmon Dip

- *300g pkt smoked salmon, finely chopped*
- *2 tbs. cream*
- *1 tsp. horseradish cream*
- *1 tsp. chives chopped*

Combine all and mix well.

Optional: Pile onto thick slices of Lebanese cucumber or Lebanese bread.

Salad Dressings

What you focus on most you attract, so make each thought count towards your betterment rather than your detriment.

Rachael Bermingham

Balsamic & Garlic Dressing

- *2 tbs. balsamic vinegar*
- *¼ cup lemon juice*
- *1 clove crushed garlic*
- *¾ cup olive oil*

Combine all ingredients in a screw-top jar and shake well.

Cocktail Sauce

- *½ cup mayonnaise*
- *½ cup tomato sauce*
- *½ tsp. worcestershire sauce*
- *2 tbs. cream*

Combine all ingredients in a bowl and stir well. Season with sea salt and pepper.

Easy Thai Dressing

- *2 tbs. sugar*
- *2 tbs. lime juice*
- *1/3 cup fish sauce*
- *Chilli powder to taste*

Combine all ingredients in a screw-top jar and shake well.

Greek Yoghurt & Whole Egg Mayonnaise

This is absolutely SENSATIONAL; *will make a salad eater of anyone!!!*

- *2/3 part natural Greek yoghurt*
- *1/3 part whole egg mayonnaise*

Mix well, season with salt and pepper and serve over salad.

Honey Mustard Dressing

- *2 tsp. honey*
- *1.5 tbs. dijon mustard*
- *2 tbs. white wine vinegar*
- *½ cup extra virgin olive oil*

Place honey and mustard in a small bowl; season with sea salt and pepper. Add vinegar and stir with a fork until completely dissolved. Slowly pour in oil while whisking vigorously. Taste and adjust seasonings, if necessary.

Potato Salad Dressing

A recipe from the very talented Verna Day.

- *½ cup cream cheese*
- *2/3 cup sour cream*
- *1 tbs. chopped mint*
- *1 tbs. sweet chilli sauce*

Combine all with an electric mixer and pour over potatoes (makes one cup).

Spinach & Strawberry Salad Dressing

- *1/3 cup balsamic vinegar*
- *2/3 cup extra virgin olive oil*
- *2 tsp. caster sugar*
- *1 tbs. fresh chives, finely chopped*

Combine dressing ingredients in a jar, adding 1 tbs. of water and salt and pepper to taste. Shake really, really well. Taste and adjust seasonings, if required.

Tomato Pickle Dressing

- *½ cup mayonnaise*
- *2 tbs. tomato pickle*
- *1 tbs. dijon mustard*

Mix ingredients together until combined. Serve with grilled fish.

Vinaigrette

- *½ cup olive oil*
- *½ cup white-wine vinegar*
- *¼ cup finely chopped fresh flat-leaf parsley*
- *2 tsp. dijon mustard*

Combine all ingredients in a screw-top jar and shake well.

Wasabi Dressing

**A recipe by Tanya Ormsby owner of the dynamic :
www.zanaproductions.com.au**

- *2 tsp. wasabi*
- *1/3 cup lemon juice*
- *1/3 cup peanut oil*
- *2 tsp. finely chopped fresh dill*

Combine all ingredients in a screw-top jar and shake well.

Sauces

An eye for an eye, leaves the whole world blind

Gandhi

Barbequed Stir Fry Sauce

- ½ cup BBQ Sauce
- 2 tsp. prepared minced ginger
- 2 tbs. soy sauce

Simply mix; absolutely delicious in a beef stir-fry.

Beer Batter

- 1 cup beer
- 1 cup plain flour
- 2 egg whites

Whisk egg whites until light and fluffy. Place flour and a pinch of sea salt in a bowl, mix in beer until smooth and lump free. Fold in egg whites and allow to stand for 10-15 minutes before using.

Best Gravy Ever

- *2 heaped tbs. Maggi rich gravy mix*
- *2 cups water*

Heat 1.5 cups of water in saucepan, mix remaining water with gravy until lump free and add to saucepan. Stir continuously until thick. If you cannot find Maggi Rich Gravy Mix, use Maggi Roast Meat Gravy!

Best 'In-a-hurry' Sauce

Serve with any meat and Asian steamed vegetables.

- *1 clove garlic, crushed*
- *¼ cup sweet chilli sauce*
- *¼ cup soy sauce*
- *2 tsp. fresh ginger grated*

Combine all ingredients and mix well.

Caramel Sauce

This is heaven served over just about anything!

- *1 cup cream*
- *¾ cup brown sugar*
- *¾ cup unsalted butter*

Combine all ingredients in a small saucepan and bring to the boil over medium heat. Simmer for 2 minutes.

Chilli Mayonnaise

- *½ tsp. sambal oelek*
- *1/3 cup whole egg mayonnaise*
- *¼ tsp. ground cumin*
- *2 tbs. sour cream*

Combine all ingredients in a bowl, mix well for a delicious flavour.

Optional: Add 1 tbs. freshly chopped coriander. Delicious served with sweet potato chips

Easy Mocha Sauce

- *1 cup dark chocolate*
- *300ml thickened cream*
- *2 tsp. instant coffee*

Combine all ingredients and cook in microwave for 2 minutes, stopping to stir half way. Serve this with Wendy's Poached Pears *– simply stunning!*

Easy Satay

- *½ cup crunchy peanut butter*
- *2 tbs. sweet chilli sauce*
- *¾ cup liquid vegetable stock*
- *1 tbs. fresh coriander, chopped*

Combine peanut butter, sweet chilli sauce and stock; cook stirring continually for 2-3 minutes.   Serve in dipping plate topped with fresh coriander.

Optional: Delicious served with wedges and mezze of vegetables (cucumber, carrot, celery, cherry tomatoes, etc).

Easiest & Yummiest Satay Sauce

Introduced by Tania Pardede. It may be difficult to find but well worth the effort!

- *1 pkt Bumbu Pecal – Peanut instant salad dressing*
- *1 cup water*

Slice contents. Add ¾ cup boiling water and mix well. Add more water, if required.

Optional: Absolutely delicious served over any kind of kebab or over a stir-fry.

Garlic Butter

- ¼ cup soft butter
- 2 cloves garlic, crushed
- 1 tps. lemon juice
- ¼ tsp. parsley, finely chopped

Mix all together and season with sea salt and pepper.

Optional: Slice a French stick every 3cm and spread the garlic butter generously, cover with alfoil and bake in a moderate oven for 10 minutes.

Ginger & Mango Sauce

- 425g mangoes in juice
- ½ pkt French onion soup mix
- 1 tbs. prepared minced ginger

Puree mangoes and juice in a food processor or blender. Add onion soup mix and ginger and mix thoroughly. Pour into saucepan. Bring to boil and simmer for 5 minutes. Yummy served with meat and chicken.

Optional: Use fresh mangoes when in season.

Horseradish Cream

- ½ cup sour cream
- 2 tbs. horseradish cream
- 2 tsp. chopped shallots
- 1 tsp. white balsamic or white-wine vinegar

Combine sour cream, horseradish cream, shallots and vinegar in small bowl. Refrigerate until ready to serve.

Horseradish, Mustard & Walnut Cream Sauce

- 250g low-fat sour cream
- 1 tbs. dijon mustard
- ¼ cup horseradish cream
- ½ cup roasted walnuts, finely chopped

Mix all ingredients well. Lovely served with fish or chicken.

Mango Salsa

- 1 cup mango flesh, cubed
- 1 lime
- ½ red finger chilli
- 3 stems of fresh coriander, finely chopped

Cut the lime in half, juice and zest one half. Cut chilli in half, remove the seeds and chop very finely. Combine all ingredients adding sea salt and pepper to taste. Serve with grilled fish or prawns.

Mixed Berry Sauce

- ½ cup cream
- ¼ cup brown sugar firmly packed
- 1 cup frozen mixed berries

Heat cream and sugar, stirring until sugar dissolves. Add mixed berries and cook, stirring for 2 minutes. Cool before spooning over vanilla ice-cream or basic cheesecake.

Mustard Sauce

- ¼ cup sour cream
- ¼ cup mayonnaise
- 2 tbs. dry mustard
- 1.5 tbs. vinegar

Combine all sauce ingredients and mix well. Heat in the microwave just prior to serving.

Onion Jam

- 3 large Spanish onions
- 3 tbs. balsamic vinegar
- ½ cup brown sugar
- 2 tbs. extra virgin olive oil

Slice onion into thin strips. Add onion to a pre-heated pot and cook until completely collapsed. Add vinegar and sugar and stir in well; turn pot down to a low heat. Leave on low heat until a jam-like consistency, stirring occasionally.

Optional: This is a great topper on steak.

Pesto Pleasure

- *½ cup low-fat sour cream*
- *¼ cup basil pesto*

Mix together. Serve with pasta, potatoes or steamed green vegetables such as asparagus or broccoli.

Soy, Ginger Dipping Sauce

- *1/3 cup soy sauce*
- *2 tsp. white sugar*
- *1-2 cm piece ginger, grated*

Combine all in a small saucepan, stir over low heat until the sugar dissolves.

Optional: This is d.e.l.i.c.i.o.u.s served with honey and orange prawns.

Tempura Batter

- *2/3 cup plain flour*
- *1/3 cup corn flour*
- *¾ can soda water (real cold)*

Sift flours in a bowl and add a pinch of sea salt. Make a well in the center and add soda water, mix well until smooth and lump free. Set aside for 10-15 minutes before using.

Optional: Use small cut vegetables and meats and shallow fry.

White Sauce

- 2 tbs. butter
- 2 tbs. flour
- 1 cup milk

Melt butter in saucepan and remove from heat. Stir in flour and blend in milk. Return to heat, stir until sauce boils and thickens, and simmer for 2 minutes. Season with sea salt and pepper and add extra milk if required.

Yoghurt Dipping Sauce

A lovely healthy accompaniment to any Indian flavoured dish.

- ¾ cup natural yoghurt
- 1 medium Lebanese cucumber
- 2 tbs. lemon juice
- 1 tbs. mint leaves

Combine all in a serving bowl.

Cocktail Food

"Every person is a new door to a different world."

From the movie "Six Degrees of Separation"
(thanks to Steve's Famous Quotes)

Asparagus Canapés

A recipe from Wendy Beattie, like the lady…Absolutely Fabulous!

- *2 bunches asparagus*
- *125g camembert*
- *100g prosciutto*

Cut the bottom off each asparagus spear and rinse. Cut 3cm strips of prosciutto with scissors. Cut half of the camembert wheel into long, thin strips. Lay prosciutto flat horizontally, place one asparagus spear vertically on the meat. Lay a slice of camembert along the asparagus and roll the prosciutto around its contents. Place on a baking tray and bake in a 150C oven until the cheese has melted. Serve immediately.

Apricots & Blue Cheese

Santa will LOOOOOVE these!!

- *6 large fresh apricots*
- *Small block mild blue cheese*
- *12 walnuts, chopped*

Halve and stone small apricots and stuff with the mild blue cheese and walnuts.

Baked Brie with Peaches

- *250g brie cheese*
- *2 tbs. raspberry jam*
- *1 cup fresh peaches, peeled and diced*
- *1 tbs. brown sugar*

Preheat oven to 180C. Place brie in small shallow baking dish and evenly spread with jam. Top with peaches and sprinkle with brown sugar. Bake for 10-12 minutes or until the cheese softens.

Optional: Serve with crackers and French bread slices.

Beer Battered Poppy seed Bread

- *1 pkt wholemeal bread mix*
- *1 bottle of beer*
- *3 tbs. butter*
- *1 tsp. of poppy seeds*

Preheat oven to 180C. Combine (knead) all ingredients in a bowl. Turn batter into a greased and floured bread tin. Bake for 50 minutes or until bread springs back upon pressing with your fingertip.

Brie Bruschetta

- *1 crusty French stick, sliced 1 inch thick*
- *6-8 ripe tomatoes, chopped*
- *250g brie cheese*

Under grill, toast one side of the French bread slices. Remove and turn slices over. Brush untoasted side with some of the juices that result when you chop the tomatoes. Lay slices of brie on the bread. Grill for a further 2-3 minutes until cheese is melted. Top with tomatoes and season with sea salt and pepper.

Cheese Pies

These little melt-in-the-mouth pies are best eaten warm.

- *2 sheets puff pastry*
- *200g mozzarella, grated*
- *200g feta cheese*
- *2 eggs, lightly beaten (reserve a little for basting)*

Cut the pastry in half, roll out until you can cut 16 rounds with a 10cm pastry cutter (We used a cup). Place aside. In a bowl, mash the feta cheese with a fork, mix in mozzarella and then add the eggs. Put a tablespoon of the filling on one half of each round of pastry. Slightly dampen the pastry edges then fold the pastry over the filling to make a half-moon shape. Seal the pies by pressing down with the prongs of a fork and brush with reserved beaten egg for a presentable finish.

Place on sheets of alfoil on a baking tray and bake them in a pre-heated oven at 200C for 15-20 minutes, or until they are puffed and golden.

Curried Eggs

- *6 hardboiled eggs*
- *2 tbs. whole egg mayonnaise*
- *½ tsp. curry powder*
- *½ tsp. parsely, finely chopped*

Peel eggs and cut in half lengthwise. Remove yolks and mash. Add mayonnaise, curry powder, parsley and season with sea salt and pepper. Place yolk mixture back into the egg halves and chill before serving.

Fried Camembert

This is sooooo easy and a real crowd pleaser!

- *250g camembert cheese*
- *1 egg*
- *4 tbs. fine breadcrumbs*
- *1 cup vegetable oil*

Cut chilled cheese into equal wedges. Lightly beat the egg and dip each cheese wedge, turning to coat. Roll in breadcrumbs. Cover and refrigerate. Deep-fry, turning regularly until golden brown in colour.

Optional: Add same quantity of sesame seeds to breadcrumbs for a little crunch. Serve with cranberry sauce (you can buy it from any supermarket).

Honey & Orange Prawns

A recipe by Susan Smith …go girlfriend!

- *24 king prawns, cooked*
- *2 tsp. olive oil*
- *2 tbs. honey*
- *1 orange*

Peel and de-vein prawns. With the orange, finely grate 1 tbs. of zest and reserve 2 tbs. of orange juice. Combine oil, rind, juice and half the honey in a bowl; add prawns and marinade in the fridge for 1 hour. Cook in a hot, non-stick frypan until golden brown.

Optional: Serve with soy, ginger dipping sauce.

Hummus & Salad Tarts

A recipe from Kendra Horwood.

- *6 mini pastry cases*
- *1 cup hummus*
- *1.5 cups mixed salad leaves (incl. herbs and edible flowers)*
- *1 tbs. lemon juice*

Combine lemon and salad, season with salt and pepper. Fill shells with hummus and pile the salad on top.

Mango Prawns

- *300g medium sized prawns, cooked*
- *2 stems of fresh basil leaves*
- *1 fresh mango*
- *100g prosciutto*

Peel medium size, cooked prawns. De-vein and cut prawns down the vein line, careful not to cut through. Flatten prawns slightly and lay a small basil leaf and sliver of mango over each prawn. Cut 2cm strips of prosciutto with scissors, wrap around each prawn and secure with a cocktail stick.

Optional: Rachael did these on soaked skewers and baked in 180C oven for 5 minutes, she sprinkled with chopped basil at the end and they were scrumptious!

Marinated & Baked Olives

- *500g green olives, pitted*
- *1 lemon peel only*
- *2 sprigs rosemary*
- *2 cloves garlic, thinly sliced*

Preheat oven to 200C. Place olives in a baking dish and with a rolling pin, gently push down so skin splits. Mix in the lemon peel, rosemary and garlic. Cook for 15 minutes and serve warm.

Optional: Add 1 tbs. olive oil to the mix.

Mozzarella Cubes

- *250g block mozzarella*
- *2 eggs*
- *1 cup Jatz bickies, crumbed*
- *¼ cup extra virgin olive oil*

Cut mozzarella into 3cm cubes. Lightly beat the eggs, dip the cheese cubes into the egg and then into the Jatz bickie crumbs (for best result, put your bickies through your food processor). Heat the oil in a frying pan and fry the cheese until golden brown.

Optional: Serve with sweet chilli sauce.

Nin's Easy & Tasty Mushrooms

A recipe from Jan Neale, these are really easy and really nice!

- *12 medium sized mushrooms*
- *Sweet chilli sauce*
- *Brie cheese*

Wash mushrooms and de-stalk. Place a dollop of sweet chilli sauce in the middle and top with a sliver of brie cheese. Place under warmed grill until brie melts.

Optional: Garnish with fresh herbs.

Quesadilla

Spanish and Speedy – *sensational served with a corona and lime!!*

- *4 flour tortilla*
- *4 tbs. tahini*
- *2 cups mozzarella, grated*
- *4 tsp. mixed herbs*

On flour tortillas, smear tahini and season with sea salt and pepper. Sprinkle on mozzarella and mixed herbs. Fold tortilla in half. Place in a preheated oven 150C and, when cooked, cut into wedges and serve.

Optional: Serve with salsa as a dipping sauce.

Sharchos (cousin of Nachos)

A t.e.r.r.i.f.i.c recipe from Sharon Webby.

* *250g cream cheese*
* *420g can baked beans with sweet chilli sauce*
* *¾ cup cheddar cheese, grated*
* *Corn chips*

In a serving dish spread the cream cheese, top with the baked beans and sprinkle with cheese. Place under the grill until the cheese bubbles and is golden/brown in colour. Serve warm with corn chips ... *Enjoy*!

Salmon Pittas

A timeless canapé from Kendra Horwood.

* *Mini pitta breads*
* *1 pkt smoked salmon*
* *1 tub crème fraîche*
* *Watercress*

Depending on size of your pittas, if quite thick cut in half. Top with smoked salmon, a dollop of crème fraîche and watercress to garnish.

Savoury Scrolls

A recipe from the beautiful Lisa Darr.

- 1 sheet puff pastry
- 2 rashers bacon
- 2 tbs. tomato paste or pizza paste
- ¼ cup parmesan cheese

Smooth tomato paste over the sheet of pastry. Scatter chopped bacon and cheese. Roll into log. Cut into pinwheels (3cm thick) and bake 180C for 15 minutes, or until pastry turns a golden brown.

Spinach Cob

A beauty from Jocelyn Wilson.

- 1 cob loaf
- 2 x 250g tubs lite sour cream
- 1 pkt spring & vegetable soup
- 1 bunch fresh spinach or alternatively, a 250g pkt frozen spinach

Boil enough spinach leaves to fill a cup, drain and allow to cool slightly. Mix sour cream, soup mix and spinach. Cook in microwave for 5 minutes. Combine and let favours develop for 15 minutes. Cut lid off your cob, scoop out the filling. Pour mixture into the cob and serve, using the scooped filling to dip.

Strawberry Camembert Sticks

- *½ cup balsamic vinegar*
- *1 punnet strawberries, washed and hulled*
- *125g camembert*
- *Short bamboo skewers*

Simmer about ½ cup balsamic vinegar in a small pan until reduced by half and syrupy. Leave to cool. Thread small strawberries onto skewers with small wedges of camembert alternately.
Drizzle balsamic syrup over strawberries just before serving.

Strawberry Sweet & Sour

A recipe from Lorraine Leeson ...
This will make an impact – TRY IT!!!

- *1 punnet strawberries, washed*
- *¼ cup brown sugar*
- *½ cup of lite sour cream*

Place brown sugar and sour cream in separate ramekins, dip a strawberry into sour cream and then into the sugar ... Savour the Flavour!

Tandoori Wings

d.e.l.i.c.i.o.u.s

- *1 kg chicken wings*
- *1/3 cup tandoori paste*
- *1/3 cup yoghurt*
- *1 medium brown onion grated*

Preheat oven to 200C. Combine paste, yoghurt and onion in large bowl. Add chicken and coat generously. Cover and refrigerate for at least 3 hours. Place chicken on an oiled wire rack set inside larger shallow baking dish. Roast, uncovered, in hot oven about 30 minutes, or until chicken is well browned and cooked through.

Tangy Cheese Balls

- *½ cup cream cheese softened*
- *¼ cup blue cheese finely crumbled*
- *2 tbs. orange zest*
- *1/3 cup mixed nuts finely chopped*

Combine cream cheese, blue cheese and orange zest. Form into small balls and roll in nuts. Chill for an hour, or until firm, and serve.

Spanish Omelette

- *500g potatoes*
- *4 eggs*
- *2 tbs. extra virgin olive oil*
- *1 onion, grated*

Peel the potatoes, wash them thoroughly and cut into thin slices, season with sea salt. Heat oil in a frying pan and add the salted potatoes. Stir them until they are slightly browned. Add the onion and let it fry for 3 or 4 minutes. Beat the eggs and add the fried potatoes. Mix well. Cook them on high. Brown on one side and then turn, to brown the other.

Spinach & Ricotta Scrolls

A recipe from Wendy Beattie.   Excellent entertainers!

- *250g frozen chopped spinach, thawed*
- *1/2 cup ricotta cheese*
- *1 cup mozzarella or cheddar cheese, grated*
- *3 sheets puff pastry*

Combine spinach, which has been lightly squeezed to remove any excess water, and cheeses and mix well. Season with sea salt and pepper. Halve each pastry sheet lengthways, then cut each piece diagonally so you have 12 long triangular strips. Place a heaped tablespoon of mixture at the widest end and roll to enclose. Place on baking tray and bake in 180C oven for 20 - 25 minutes or until golden.

Optional: Baste with beaten egg for a really presentable finish.

Vegetable Wontons

A healthy, popular starter for all.

- ½ cup carrot, grated
- ½ cup bean sprouts
- ½ cup of chopped/shredded vegetables of choice (sweet potato, zucchini, mushroom, cabbage are some great options)
- 1 pkt of Wonton Wrappers (around 10 papers)

Combine all ingredients and place a teaspoon of mixture along the centre of each of the wonton papers. Roll up into small spring roll sized rolls, tucking in the sides as you roll. Steam for 6-8 minutes in a vegetable steamer. Serve warm.

Optional: Serve with Sweet Chilli Sauce.

Morning & Afternoon Teas

Everyone smiles in the same language
Anonymous

Almond Bread Slice

Makes 15 slices. Recipe from Cyndi O'Meara.

- *4 organic free range eggwhites*
- *½ cup organic raw sugar*
- *1 cup organic unbleached flour*
- *1 cup almonds*

Preheat oven to 180C. Beat eggwhites until stiff, then add sugar and beat for 1 minute. Stir in flour and almonds. Place mixture in a greased or lined loaf tin and bake for 40 minutes. When cool enough, slice thinly. Place slices on a baking tray and return to oven until browned (10-15 minutes).

Caramel Ginger Tarts

**Makes 12. A recipe from the gifted Jennette McCosker
… Easy and Economical!**

- *12 ginger nut bickies*
- *400g can Nestle Top n Fill caramel*
- *½ tub cream - whipped*
- *1 banana*

Place cookies on the individual circles of a patty cake tin and bake in 150C oven for 10 minutes. Remove and gently mould the softened bickies into patty cake tin. When cool, add enough caramel to fill the bickie. Top with whipped cream and a slice or two of banana as garnish.

Chocolate Parcels

Makes 25. Recipe from Cyndi O'Meara … Y.U.M!

- *1 cup dark cooking chocolate*
- *1 cup slivered almonds, lightly roasted*
- *½ cup chopped glazed ginger*

Melt chocolate in a double boiler, stirring constantly. Remove from heat as soon as completely melted. Add roasted almonds and ginger to the melted chocolate and mix well. Spoon small amounts 2cm apart on a lined baking tray. Refrigerate until hardened and serve. Store parcels in an airtight container and refrigerate.

Cream Cheese Icing

- *1 tbs. butter*
- *2-3 tbs. cream cheese*
- *1 tsp. lemon rind grated (optional)*
- *1-1.5 cups icing sugar*

Soften butter. Add cream cheese and beat well. Add lemon rind and sifted icing sugar (start with 1 cup and if you need more add slowly). Continue to beat until icing is nice and smooth.

Crostoli

A recipe from Jan Neale 'Nin'. These are delicious, served with coffee.

- *1 sheet shortcrust pastry*
- *1 cup vegetable oil*
- *¼ cup caster sugar and cinnamon sugar combined*

Cut pastry into 1.5 cm strips twist and place on a baking tray. Freeze for 10-15 minutes. Heat oil on high; it is ready when a piece of pastry sizzles in it. Deep-fry the twists in batches, turning once until golden. Remove and place on draining paper. Whilst hot, coat well with the castor and cinnamon sugar mix.

Optional: Dust with icing sugar for presentation

Coconut Macaroons

Makes 25-30. Recipe from Lisa Hayes.

- *2 eggs, separated*
- *¾ cup organic sugar*
- *3 cups organic coconut*

Preheat oven to 180C. Add a pinch of salt to eggwhites, and beat until soft peaks form. Beat in egg yolks one at a time; gradually add sugar, beating well after each addition. Stir in coconut and mix well. Spoon tablespoons of mixture onto foil lined trays. Bake for 8 minutes, or until golden brown.

Delicious Fruit Cake

Serves 4. Recipe from Jen Whittington. Delicious & nutritious!

- *1kg mixed fruit*
- *2 cups fruit juice/cold organic tea of choice*
- *1 tbs. sherry, or similar*
- *2 cups organic self raising flour*

Preheat oven to 125C. Soak fruits in juice/tea and sherry for 2 hours. Stir flour into soaked fruit and mix well. Put into large lined baking tin. Bake for 2 hours in the bottom of your oven on 130C. Remove and leave to cool. Put into container or wrap in foil. Keep for 2 – 3 days before cutting.

Optional: Instead of sherry we have used Cointreau and Grand Marnier ... mmm!

Easy Pecan Pie

Serves 6. This is really easy and really nice!

- *3 eggwhites*
- *1 cup caster sugar*
- *1 cup pecans, chopped*
- *22 Jatz bickies, crushed*

Beat eggwhites until stiff, gently adding caster sugar throughout. Fold in chopped pecan nuts and crushed Jatz bickies. Pour mixture into a pie dish and bake in a moderate oven for 25 min.

Optional: Add a dash of vanilla essence with the jatz. Slice as you would a cheesecake and top with a dollop of whipped cream and piece of seasonal fruit.

Easy Pineapple Cake

A recipe by Brett McCosker.   2 words – *TRY IT!!!*

- *2 cups self raising flour*
- *1 cup sugar*
- *450g can crushed pineapple*

Sift flour into a mixing bowl and combine with sugar. Add pineapple and mix well. Pour into a greased cake tin and bake at 180C for 40 minutes.

Optional: For best result bake in a ring cake tin.

Easy Pineapple Cake Icing

- *400g can condensed milk*
- *⅓ cup butter melted*
- *1 cup shredded coconut*
- *½ tsp. vanilla*

Combine condensed milk and melted margarine and bring to boil. Stirring constantly, boil for 4 minutes. Add coconut and mix. While mixture is hot, spread over cooled cake.

Optional: The above amounts cover the entire cake, lid and sides. If, however, you just want to cover the lid use half of the ingredients.

Easy Vanilla Pie

- *1 cup lite sour cream*
- *1 cup milk*
- *1 pkt vanilla instant pudding*
- *1 pkt biscuit base mix*

Beat sour cream and milk until smooth, add the pudding mix and continue beating slowly until mixture thickens. Pour into pre-made biscuit base mix and chill for an hour.

Optional: Serve with a dollop of whipped cream and fruit of your choice.

Flourless Chocolate Cake

- *4 eggs*
- *200g butter*
- *200g dark chocolate*
- *1 cup caster sugar*

Preheat oven 180C. Separate eggs; add ½ the sugar to the yolks and beat well with a mixer. Beat egg whiles until fluffy then add remaining sugar, gradually beating until stiff peaks form. Melt butter and chocolate over hot water stirring regularly. Pour into egg yolk mixture and fold. Once combined fold in egg whites. Line a cake tin with greaseproof paper and pour in mixture. Bake for 40 minutes in the lower third of your oven. NB: This cake will collapse, as it has no flour to sustain the rise.

Optional: Can be served warm or cold and is delicious with fresh whipped cream.

Gingered Prunes

Serves 4. By Jocelyn Wilson … these are real treats!!

- *1 pkt prunes, pips removed*
- *¾ tub cream*
- *1 small pkt crystallised ginger*
- *1 tbs. icing sugar*

Finely dice the crystallised ginger. Combine cream, ginger and icing sugar. Fill the centre of prunes.

Honey Joys

- *3 tbs. butter*
- *1/3 cup sugar*
- *1 tbs. honey*
- *4 cups cornflakes*

Preheat oven 150C. Heat butter, sugar and honey in small saucepan till frothy, remove from heat. Add cornflakes and mix well. Spoon into patty cake cases and bake for 10 minutes.

Jam Tarts

- *1 sheet ready rolled sweet short-pastry*
- *1 tbs. butter*
- *Your choice of jam*

Lay pastry flat and cut as many circles as possible; press each circle into a lightly buttered patty cake tin, pressing a fork down around the edges for decoration. Cook at 180C for around 10 minutes. Spoon the desired amount of jam into each tart, return to the oven for another 5 minutes.

Optional: Top with a dollop of freshly whipped cream

Kisses

- *½ cup butter, reserve a tsp.*
- *1 cup self raising flour*
- *1 tbs. organic icing sugar*
- *1 tbs. organic arrowroot*

Preheat oven to 150C. Cream butter and sugar and add arrowroot and flour. Grease a baking tray with reserved butter, scoop a teaspoon full onto tray and press with a fork. Cook till pale brown.

Optional: Join 2 together with some jam when cold.

Lime & Macadamia Fudge

- *395g can condensed milk*
- *500g white chocolate melts*
- *150g macadamia nuts, chopped*
- *2 limes, zest finely grated*

Line an 18cm square tin with baking paper. Place condensed milk and melts in a saucepan and stir over a low heat until smooth then remove from heat. Add nuts and zest and mix well. Pour into tin and refrigerate overnight prior to cutting.

Mandarin & Almond Cake

And who says you learn nothing at Work Conferences... Thanks, Fiona Burt!

- *3 mandarins*
- *1 cup sugar*
- *6 eggs*
- *2 cups almond meal*

Cover mandarins with water, bring to boil then simmer for 1 hour. Cool completely, then remove seeds, and puree. Beat eggs and sugar together, add puree and almond meal. Stir well, pour into greased cake tin and bake at 160C for 70 minutes.

Optional: Kelly Mauger, a 'Dynamite Chef' at Bella Boo Café in Mundubbera, QLD advised that you can substitute mandarins with apples, bananas or oranges. I made it with oranges and topped with cream cheese icing...BEEEEEUUUUUUUTIFUL!!

Meringues

- *2 eggwhites*
- *½ cup caster sugar*
- *¼ tsp. vanilla*
- *1 tbs. butter*

Preheat oven 150C. Whip eggwhites till stiff then gradually add sugar and vanilla, continuing to beat. Place in dessert spoonfuls onto well greased, with butter, baking tray. Bake in oven until dry and firm.

For Best Result: If eggwhites are allowed to stand overnight they will whip up more quickly. A pinch of salt in eggwhites makes them stiffen quickly. To prevent a meringue topping shrinking and boooming moist after cooking, sift a dusting of icing sugar over the meringue before placing in the oven.

Meg's Decadent Chocolate Lychees

A recipe from Meg Wilson. These are elegant, quick, easy & amazing with coffee.

- *½ cup milk chocolate*
- *¼ cup cream*
- *1.5 cups fresh lychees, peeled and de-pipped*

Melt chocolate add ¼ cup of cream and mix well.
Dip lychees & set in fridge.

Peanut Butter Cookies

Makes around 20

- *1 cup crunchy peanut butter*
- *1 cup sugar*
- *1 tsp. cinnamon*
- *1 large egg*

Preheat oven to 180C. Mix all ingredients into a bowl. Spoon small tablespoon sized balls onto 2 lined baking trays. Slightly flatten with a fork, crisscross style. Bake for 8 minutes, or until a thin crust forms on the cookie.

Optional: Robyn Mayeke suggested that these work just as well without cinnamon, stores well and kids love them!

Rum Balls I

Makes 15. An absolute treasure from Anthony 'Spud' Moore.

- *500g moist Christmas cake or heavy fruit cake*
- *½ cup dark rum*
- *250g dark chocolate*
- *1 cup desiccated coconut*

Place Christmas cake and rum in a food processor and blend until combined. Allow to stand for 30 minutes in fridge. Melt chocolate. Roll cake mix into balls, smother with chocolate and roll in coconut. Place on a tray and chill before serving.

Rum Balls II

Thanks for the idea Russell Halfpenny.

- *2.5 cups crushed weet bix*
- *3 tbs. dark rum*
- *400g can condensed milk*
- *¾ cup desiccated coconut*

Mix all ingredients, except ¼ cup of coconut. Add rum and condensed milk. Mix thoroughly (add extra weet bix if required). Shape into balls and roll in extra coconut. Store in fridge.

Optional: Add 1 cup of mixed fruit to the dry ingredients and reduce weet bix quantity to 2 cups.

Scones

Makes 12. A recipe from the kitchen wonder herself, Daphne Beutel; *it doesn't get any easier!*

- *4 cups self raising flour*
- *300ml cream*
- *1 can lemonade*

Sift self raising flour into a bowl, make a well and pour in cream and lemonade. Mix to make a firm dough, roll out, cut with a scone cutter and bake in hot oven until golden brown.

Shortbread

A recipe by the lovely Jennette McCosker.

- *½ cup butter*
- *½ cup plain flour*
- *3 tbs. cornflour*
- *3 tbs. icing sugar*

Preheat oven to 180C. Mix altogether in a blender. Press into baking tray lined with baking paper. Bake for 30 minutes.

Ultimate Caramel Macadamia Tart

Rach's Dad, Billy Moore's absolute favourite.

- *1 sheet short crust pastry*
- *400g can Nestle Top n Fill caramel*
- *100g dark cooking chocolate*
- *18 macadamia nuts, roasted*

Preheat oven to 180C. Cut pastry into 4 squares and mould into greased muffin tin. Bake for 5-10 minutes, or until lightly golden brown. Melt chocolate and brush pastry shells internally. Spoon the caramel into the shells and top with the roasted macadamia nuts.

White Chocolate Spiders

Makes 12. A recipe by Lorraine Leeson ... D.e.l.i.c.i.o.u.s!

- 100g pkt Chang's original fried noodles
- 2 tbs. crunchy peanut butter
- 200g pkt white chocolate

Microwave chocolate and peanut butter for 1 minute. Mix well until smooth. Add noodles and coat generously. Spoon the mixture onto a lined baking tray and refrigerate until set.

Optional: White can be substituted with dark chocolate for a nice change.

Light Meals & Lunches

Soups

Worries go down better with soup.

Jewish Proverb

Asparagus Soups

Serves 4-6

- *400g can asparagus tips*
- *440g can cream of chicken soup*

Mix all ingredients plus 1 cup of water, heat until boiling. Serve with toasted bread fingers and a few asparagus tips as garnish.

Chilled Melon Soup

Serves 6. A real delight on a hot summer night!

- *1 medium rock melon*
- *½ honeydew melon*
- *½ cup sparkling grape juice chilled (available all supermarkets)*
- *6 strawberries washed, hulled and quartered*

Blend rock melon in food processor until smooth. Add sparkling grape juice and blend quickly to combine. Serve immediately in bowls with diced honeydew, strawberries and crushed ice.

Kim's French Onion Soup

Serves 2

- *2 large onions, peeled and coarsely chopped*
- *2 zucchinis, coarsely chopped*
- *1 pkt French onion soup*
- *½ cup cream*

Place onions, zucchinis and soup mix in a saucepan with 4 cups of water, season with pepper and boil, reduce heat by half and leave for 30 minutes stirring occasionally. Blend till smooth, add cream, stir and serve.

Optional: Grill some tasty cheese on a thick slice of French stick and place in middle of the soup before serving.

Pea & Ham Soup

Serves 4-6

- *3 cups of chicken stock*
- *3 cups of frozen peas*
- *5 fresh sage leaves*
- *1 ham steak*

Bring stock to boil. Add peas and sage leaves and cook for 5 minutes. Place in a blender or food processor and process until smooth. Return to saucepan. Remove rind from ham. Chop flesh very finely. Mix into soup and bring to the boil.

Optional: Serve hot with crusty bread.

Pumpkin Soup

Serves 4-6. A recipe from Lisa Darr.
Fabulously fast and flavoursome!

- *½ jap pumpkin, skinned & thinly sliced*
- *5 chicken stock cubes*
- *1 large brown onion*
- *Enough water to cover pumpkin*

Boil all ingredients until soft. Blend until smooth.

Optional: Serve with a generous dollop of sour cream.

Salmon & Asparagus Soup

Serves 6. A recipe from Alexis Wallis.
An amazing entertainer for very little effort!

- *440g can cream of asparagus soup*
- *220g can red salmon*
- *300 ml cream*

Drain salmon, removing skin and bones before pureeing in a blender. In a saucepan, mix blended salmon with cream of asparagus soup and 1 cup water. Add cream to the mixture, heat without boiling, season with sea salt and pepper if needed.

Sweet Potato & Pear Soup

Serves 4-6

- *1 large sweet potato (white flesh, purple jacket)*
- *2 medium pears*
- *2 chicken stock cubes*

Peel and chop sweet potato and pears, place in a saucepan, cover with water and stock cubes. Cook until softened, cool slightly before blending.

Thai Pumpkin Soup

Serves 4. A recipe from Spud. *THAI-RRIFIC!!*

- *1kg butternut pumpkin, peeled and diced*
- *2 tbs. red curry paste*
- *300ml coconut cream*
- *¼ cup coriander chopped*

Sauté pumpkin and red curry paste until it starts to catch on the saucepan. Add coconut cream to deglaze the pan, top with enough water to level with the pumpkin and bring to boil. Reduce heat simmering until the pumpkin becomes soft and mushy. Puree, season with sea salt and pepper and fold in chopped coriander.

Vitamin C Soup

Serves 4. Another from Kim's very clever Mummy, Jennette McCosker.

- *425g can cream of tomato soup*
- *1 orange*
- *3 tbs. cream*

Juice the orange and then finely grate the rind. Place soup in a saucepan. Combine orange juice and sufficient water to make one can of liquid, and add to soup. Stir in orange rind and bring soup to boil. Remove from heat, stir in cream and serve immediately.

Zucchini Soup

Serves 2. A recipe from Jen Whittington.

- *1 zucchini*
- *1 onion, peeled and coarsely chopped*
- *1 pkt chicken soup*

Boil the vegetables together for 30 minutes. Drain half the water, add the dry soup and blend till smooth. Season with pepper and serve.

All Others

After 30, a body has a mind of its own.

Bette Midler

Antipasto Tart

Makes 12 and are scrumptious!

- *2 sheets puff pastry*
- *250g antipasto mix*
- *3 eggs*
- *300ml sour cream*

Use a large cup to cut 12 circles into your puff pastry sheets. Line a Tupperware muffin tray with the cut pastry (these don't require greasing). Divide the antipasto mix between each. Lightly whisk eggs, add sour cream, season with sea salt and pepper. Pour over tarts and bake in a moderate oven for 20 minutes.

Optional: Add a splash of tomato and worcestershire sauces to the egg mix. Top with a sprinkle of parmesan cheese.

Bacon Pizza

Serves 1. A recipe from the delightful Veronica Griffin.

- *1 piece of pita or Lebanese bread*
- *3 tbs. pizza sauce*
- *3 rashers bacon*
- *¼ cup mozzarella cheese*

Finely dice bacon and fry for 2 minutes. Spread pizza sauce on pita bread, sprinkle with bacon and top with mozzarella cheese. Place in a moderate oven under the grill until the cheese browns.
To maintain crisp bread, place directly onto oven racks.

Basil Polenta

Serves 1. A recipe from Spud.

- *1 cup polenta*
- *1 cup butter*
- *1 cup parmesan cheese, grated*
- *½ cup basil, chopped*

Place 4 cups of water in a saucepan and boil. Sprinkle polenta in and stir thoroughly until mixture becomes thick (10-15 minutes). Add butter and parmesan, stir gently for a further 3 minutes, fold in basil, season well and serve.

Optional: For a creamier polenta add 1 cup of cream.

Beef Koftas

Makes 4-6

- *½ cup crunchy peanut butter*
- *2 tsp. curry powder*
- *1 egg*
- *500g lean beef mince*

Warm peanut butter in the microwave on high for 30 seconds to soften. Mix in curry powder and egg. Add to mince and combine. Roll mixture into fat sausage shapes using ½ cup of mixture for each kofta. Grill or BBQ until cooked.

Optional: Serve as a burger or on pita bread with satay sauce and salad or separately as a patty with vegetables … mmmmm!

Celery Soufflé

Serves 4

- *2 tbs. butter*
- *3 tbs. flour*
- *440g can cream of celery soup*
- *4 eggs, separated*

Preheat oven to 180C. Melt butter in a saucepan and remove from heat. Stir in flour until a pasty texture. Stir in undiluted celery soup. Beat in egg yolks, one at a time. Beat eggwhites until stiff and then fold into mixture, quickly and lightly. Pour into a soufflé dish and bake for 30 −35 minutes.

Cheese & Garlic Pizza

Serves 2. A recipe from Spud.

- *3 tortilla rounds*
- *16 cloves garlic*
- *2 cups parmesan cheese, grated*
- *2 cups mozzarella, grated*

Preheat oven 230C. Peel garlic, wrap in alfoil and roast in oven for 15 minutes. Remove and cool. Lay one tortilla flat and spread 1/3 garlic, 1/3 parmesan and 1/3 mozzarella. Lay second tortilla on top and repeat process, lay third tortilla on top and repeat process. Cook for 15 minutes or until cheese bubbles and turns golden brown.

Chicken Satay Kebabs

A recipe by Tania Pardede... *SOOOO EASY & SUCH A WINNER!!!*

- *2 chicken breasts*
- *1 pkt BUMBU PECAL: Peanut Instant Salad Dressing*
- *½ cup diced cucumber*
- *Bamboo skewers, soaked*

Dice chicken and thread on skewers and grill until cooked. Slice contents of the packet into quarters and add ½ cup boiling water. Stir well. Slowly add another ½ cup boiling water or as much as is needed to reach your desired consistency. (NB: 150cc = 1 cup water.) Pour over chicken when ready to serve and top with cucumber.

Crab Cakes

This is incredibly easy and a fabulous addition to any dinner party!

- *3 cups of fresh crabmeat*
- *1 tbs. ginger, freshly grated*
- *1.75 cups plain flour*
- *5 tbs. vegetable oil*

Combine crabmeat, ginger and a little cracked pepper with flour and mix well. Divide mixture into even sized patties and place carefully in a frying pan or wok of hot oil. Cook for 2 minutes or until golden brown, remove from oil and lay on draining paper to soak up excess oil. Serve warm.

Creole Burgers

Makes 6

- *750g premium mince*
- *2 tbs. chopped parsley*
- *Rye burger roll*

Combine meat and parsley, season with sea salt and pepper and mix well. Form into 6 large patties, place under heated grill. Cook to desired doneness, turning once and leaving to sit for 5 minutes prior to serving in the roll with preferred salad.

Gourmet Pizza

Serves 1. A recipe from Karyn Turnbull-Markus, proprietor of www.deli-lightful.com.au.

- *3 tbs. Mrs. Balls peach chutney*
- *Lebanese bread*
- *3 slices prosciutto*
- *3 rounds baby bocconcini*

Spread the peach chutney over the Lebanese bread, tear prosciutto & bocconcini into strips and place on top of pizza, then place directly onto oven racks for a crispy finish and bake at 180C for 10-15 minutes.

Healthy Hamburger

Serves 4

- *4 rye bread rolls*
- *1 ½ cups cheddar cheese, grated*
- *1 cup lettuce, sliced*
- *4 organic meat patties*

Grill or BBQ meat patties. Cut rolls in half. Sprinkle cheese onto both halves of roll. Add meat patties to lower side and top with lettuce.

Healthy Hotdogs

Serves 4

- *4 wraps*
- *4 organic sausages*
- *1.5 cups of shredded cheese*
- *1 cup of shredded carrot or diced tomato or fried sliced onion*

Grill or BBQ sausages. Lay wraps out and sprinkle equal portions of cheese onto each. Add chosen vegetable and rollup.

Optional: Serve with tomato or BBQ sauce.

Jacket Potato with Tomato Salsa

Serves 1

- *1 large potato (200g)*
- *2 tbs. tomato salsa*
- *¼ cup low fat cottage cheese*
- *1 tbs. fresh chives, chopped*

Pierce potato with knife several times. Wrap potato in alfoil, bake in preheated 180C oven for 20-30 minutes, or until soft. Remove from oven, stand for 5 minutes, remove alfoil and cut a crisscross into the potato, half way through. Add cottage cheese, top with salsa and sprinkle with chives.

Oysters Kilpatrick

- *6 oysters*
- *1 bacon rasher*
- *¼ cup BBQ sauce*
- *¼ cup tomato sauce*

Preheat grill 230C. Place washed oysters on baking tray. Dice bacon finely and mix with the combined sauces. Spoon the mixture onto oysters and grill until oysters begin to bubble and bacon is crisp but not burnt.

Oysters Mexicano

- *6 oysters*
- *½ lime juiced*
- *12 corn chips*
- *¼ cup guacamole*

Place washed oysters on serving plate and pour lime evenly over them. Spoon on guacamole and stud with a corn chip for serving.

Oysters Champagne

- *6 oysters*
- *¼ tsp. minced ginger*
- *1/3 cup champagne*
- *¼ tsp. mint chopped*

Place washed oysters on serving plate. Combine remaining ingredients and spoon over oysters. Serve immediately.

Thanks Spud for the above ever-popular oyster recipes!

Salt & Pepper Calamari

Serves 6. Y.u.m.m.y!

- *1 tsp. sichuan peppercorns and 1 tsp. sea salt*
- *400g fresh calamari*
- *1 cup cornflour*
- *1 cup vegetable oil*

In a dry pan, roast the peppercorns until they become fragrant and begin to crackle, transfer to a mortar along with sea salt and grind. Add cornflour and roll the squid in the mixture, shake off any excess. Deep fry in a hot wok for 1 minute or until cooked. Drain and serve hot.

Sausage Rolls

Serves 1.   Y.u.m.m.y Y.u.m.m.y !!

- *2 sheets puff pastry*
- *250g lean mince*
- *1 onion*
- *1 tbs. flour*

Place mince and chopped onion, with slightly less than a ¼ cup of water, into a saucepan. Season generously with sea salt and pepper. Cook until mince is brown. Add flour and stir well until combined, then allow to cool. Place mince in generous spoonfuls down the centre of pastry, brush sides of pastry with water and roll up. Cut into desired thickness, place on a lined baking tray and mark tops with a knife. Bake in 180C oven for 15-20 minutes.

Optional: Add a ½ tsp. of mixed herbs to the mince mixture for flavour. Add a chopped tomato for a change. Baste pastry with milk prior to baking.

Sweet Chilli Chicken Wrap

Serves 1

- *1 wrap*
- *1 chicken thigh*
- *1 tbs. sweet chilli sauce*
- *2 tsp. soy sauce*

Chop chicken thigh into 'chunks', throw into a heated non-stick pan with sweet chilli sauce and soy sauce. Toss this mix in the hot pan until the chicken is cooked, which takes between 5-10 minutes. Heat the tortilla under a grill for 3 minutes. Once warm, place the cooked chicken on the tortilla and add whatever else you would like in the wrap.

Optional: Add fresh coriander to sweet chilli and soy sauce mix

Sweet Guacamole Wrap

Serves 4 –6. You will be pleasantly surprised!

- *1 pkt wholemeal wraps*
- *1.5 cups tasty cheese*
- *2 ripe avocados*
- *1 sweet potato*

Peel and thinly slice sweet potato. Gently steam until soft throughout then remove from heat. Spoon out avocado flesh into a small bowl, discarding shell and skin; mash flesh with a fork. Lay each wrap flat and spread 1 tbs. of avocado onto the surface, leaving an inch bare around the perimeter. Place 3 slices of the still warm sweet potato evenly onto the avocado surface. Sprinkle 2 tbs. of grated cheese onto the sweet potato. Roll wraps into logs and serve.

Vegetarian Pizza

Serves 1

- *1 wholemeal pita bread*
- *2 tbs. pizza sauce*
- *Mixed, sliced vegetables (pumpkin, onion, capsicum, eggplant, corn whatever you have in the fridge)*
- *¼ cup mozzarella cheese*

Select your vegetables, slice and grill or bake in the oven until almost soft. Spread pizza sauce on pita bread, top with vegetables and sprinkle with mozzarella cheese. Place under grill at 180C until cheese browns. For crispy bread, place pita bread directly onto oven rack.

Optional: Mix 1 tsp. basil pesto with the pizza sauce ... yummy!

Sides

Take care of your body. It's the only place you have to live.

Jim Rohn www.jrohn.com

Salads

Baby Spinach & Strawberry Salad

Serves 4

* *450g fresh baby spinach leaves*
* *2 punnets strawberries washed, hulled and sliced*
* *¾ cup sunflower seeds*
* *Spinach and strawberry salad dressing*

Place washed baby spinach in a bowl and add strawberries. Top the salad with cooled, dry-roasted sunflower seeds (spread on a baking tray and toast in a preheated oven 180C, stirring occasionally, for about 3 minutes) drizzle with suggested salad dressing.

Mango, Avocado & Bacon Salad

Serves 4. This is a *KNOCKOUT*!!

* *2 large mangoes*
* *2 avocados*
* *8 rashers of cooked, crispy bacon*

Cube mangoes and avocados, cut bacon in largish chunks and mix together in a small bowl.

Orange & Almond Salad

Serves 4

- ½ iceberg lettuce, shredded
- 2 oranges, peeled and sliced
- 4 bacon rashers
- 1/3 cup slivered almonds, toasted

Fry bacon until crispy, cool and cut roughly. Combine all ingredients in a salad bowl. Refrigerate until ready to serve.

Optional: Dress with a balsamic vinegairette.

Prawn & Avocado Salad

Serves 2

- 100g mixed lettuce
- 1 large avocado, peeled and sliced
- 200g prawns, peeled and de-veined
- 2 tbs. thousand island dressing

Arrange lettuce, avocado and prawns on two plates, drizzle with dressing.

Optional: Add 1 mango cubed and 40g macadamia nuts, lightly toasted and chopped.

Red Salad

A recipe from Perditta O'Connor; a fabulous addition to any BBQ!

- *1kg watermelon, sliced*
- *½ Spanish onion, thinly sliced*
- *2 tbs. balsamic vinegar*

Layer watermelon and onion in a serving dish and drizzle with balsamic vinegar.

Salmon & Caper Salad

Serves 4

- *100g tin drained salmon*
- *1/3 cup feta crumbled*
- *300g baby rocket (or other salad greens)*
- *1 tbs. drained capers chopped*

Simply mix and enjoy!

Thai Chilli Mango Squid Salad

Serves 4. A recipe from Spud. "This is the tastiest salad ever!" Rach

- *2 handfuls rocket lettuce*
- *500g squid cleaned*
- *1 large ripe mango*
- *250ml Thai chilli sauce*

Cut squid tubes into triangles. Marinate with Thai chilli sauce for 1 hour. De-seed and skin the mango, slice and place in a serving bowl. Pan fry squid quickly and add to mango; top with rocket and serve.

Waldorf Salad

Serves 4

- *4 cups of seasonal apples, diced*
- *¾ cup raisins*
- *½ cup pecan nuts, chopped*
- *½ cup whole egg mayonnaise*

In a bowl, combine ingredients and refrigerate until ready to serve.

Watermelon Salad

Serves 4. This is wonderful...*ABSOLUTELY sensational!!*

- *4 tbs. caramelised balsamic vinegar*
- *½ watermelon*
- *1 punnet cherry tomatoes*
- *½ cup crushed pistachios*

Cut watermelon into edible chunks, BBQ till grill marks appear on the melon. Move to a serving bowl and sprinkle with cherry tomatoes, nuts and balsamic vinegar.

Potato

Francisco Pizarro found the potato in Ecuador and brought them to Spain in the early sixteenth century!

Garlic Potato

Serves 4

- *4 large potatoes, peeled and cut into 1cm slices*
- *1 cup sour cream*
- *1.5 cups mozzarella cheese – keep ½ cup reserved*
- *2 cloves garlic, crushed*

Preheat oven 180C. Lightly steam potatoes for 15 minutes, or until just soft – set aside. Combine cheese, garlic and sour cream in a bowl. Line a baking dish with the sliced, steamed potato – keeping ¼ aside. Alternate one layer of potatoes with garlic, sour cream and cheese combination, ending with the cheese/sour cream/garlic combo. Add reserved cheese to finish off. Bake in 180C oven for 30 minutes.

Italian Herbed Potatoes

Serves 4. A recipe from Cathy Ryan. A winner at any BBQ!!

- *4 large potatoes*
- *2 tbs. olive oil*
- *1 pkt McCormick's Italian Herb Potatoes*

Peel potatoes and cut into cubes approximately 3cm x 3cm. Place the potatoes and oil in a plastic bag. Ensure an even coating. Add Italian herb mix and again coat evenly. In a preheated oven 180C, bake on a tray for 15-20 minutes or until potatoes are golden roasted and tender.

Mashed Potato with Pine Nuts

Serves 4

- *4 medium potatoes*
- *2 tbs. butter*
- *¼ cup milk*
- *1/3 cup toasted pine nuts*

Peel potatoes and cut each into 4 even pieces. Microwave potatoes until tender; drain and mash well. Add butter and milk, beating until butter is melted. Add pine nuts and mix well.

Optional: For additional flavour, add 1 tps. ground dried rosemary.

Oven Roasted Wedges

Serves 4-6. Recipe from Cyndi O'Meara.

- *6 medium potatoes, unpeeled and cut into wedges*
- *3 tbs. cold pressed macadamia nut oil*
- *1 tsp. dried oregano*
- *1 tsp. sea salt*

Preheat oven 200C. Place potatoes in a large baking dish, drizzle with oil and coat well. Bake for 20-30 minutes or until browned. Add salt and oregano, toss well and serve.

"Point it to a Window" Mashed Potatoes

Serves 4. A third generation recipe from the Wilson family.

- *4 potatoes*
- *2/3 cup of milk*

Peel potatoes. Cut in half and boil until cooked through. DO NOT over cook. Drain and place back on the cooktop. Heat the milk separately; once boiled add it to the potatoes and beat 'pointing it to a window' for the best result.

Potatoes Maxim

Serves 4-6

- *½ kg potatoes*
- *5 tbs. melted butter*

Preheat oven 200C. Peel and place the potatoes in a bowl, add the melted butter. Season with sea salt and pepper and gently mix the potatoes to coat with butter. Arrange the potatoes in a single layer on a baking tray. Place tray in the oven and bake for 30 minutes, or until the potatoes are cooked and browned.

Optional: Add 1 tbs. cumin to the seasoning

Rosemary & Thyme Potatoes

- *4 large potatoes*
- *2 tbs. olive oil*
- *1 tbs. dried or fresh rosemary*
- *1 tbs. thyme*

Preheat oven to 180C. Peel potatoes and halve. On the non-flat side, make 4 or 5 slices across the potatoes, slicing about three-quarters of the way through. Combine potatoes with oil in large baking dish, sprinkle with sea salt and pepper. Bake for approximately 20-30 minutes until potatoes are browned and tender. Mix herbs and sprinkle.

Rosemary & Mustard Mashed Potatoes

Serves 4. Kim's family's favourite mash recipe!

- *4 large potatoes*
- *2 tbs. fresh rosemary*
- *1 tbs. dijon mustard*

Boil ½ cup water with rosemary in a small saucepan. Reduce heat and simmer until infused, then drain. Boil potatoes, drain and add rosemary liquid. Mash well adding the dijon to taste.

Optional: For a creamier texture add 2 tbs. cream.

Sautéed Lemon Potatoes

Serves 4. A recipe by Michelle Dodd. *These are sensational !!*

- *4 medium potatoes*
- *½ cup lemon juice*
- *3 tbs. extra virgin olive oil*
- *1 tbs. butter*

Peel and cut potatoes into eighths, parboil for 3 minutes. Heat oil, butter and lemon juice in baking dish in a hot oven. Toss in potatoes basting with liquid and cook for 15-20 minutes or until golden.

Optional: Add freshly ground garlic to oil and lemon juice.

Simplest Potato Bake Ever

Serves 6. A recipe from Anje, Kenny Wilson's Mum *... this is fabulous!!*

- *6 potatoes*
- *300ml tub of cream*
- *1 pkt French onion soup*

Slice potatoes into 1cm thick slices, place into a baking dish. Combine cream and soup, pour over potatoes and bake in oven 180C for 30 minutes.

Stuffed Baked Potatoes

Serves 4

- *4 large washed potatoes*
- *2 cups sour cream*
- *2 cups cheese, grated*
- *2 cups of steamed vegetables*
  (mushrooms, zucchini, capsicum, squash)

Pierce potatoes with a skewer and add to a saucepan half full of boiling water. Bring to boil, cover and simmer for 15 minutes, or until just off cooked. Steam vegetables of your choice separately for 5 minutes, or until cooked. Drain potatoes and scoop about 2 tbs. of flesh from each potato and discard. Mix sour cream, cheese and vegetables together. Spoon the mixture into the hole and serve hot.

Sweet Potato Chips

Serves 4 as a side dish. Recipe from Cyndi O'Meara.

- *1 orange sweet potato*
- *3 tbs. cold pressed macadamia nut oil*
- *Sea salt*

Preheat oven to 200C. Place sweet potato in a large baking dish; drizzle with oil, coating well. Bake for 40 minutes or until browned. Sprinkle with sea salt before serving.

Vegetables

Let food be your medicine and medicine be your food.

Hippocrates

Asparagus with Butter & Parmesan

Serves 4

- *2 bunches asparagus*
- *2 tbs. melted butter*
- *½ cup parmesan cheese, shaved*

Bring water to boil in a large frying pan, add asparagus and simmer uncovered for 2 minutes and then drain. Serve drizzled with melted butter and cheese. Season with sea salt and pepper.

Asparagus with Balsamic Dressing

Serves 4

- *2 bunches asparagus*
- *4 tbs. olive oil*
- *4 tbs. balsamic vinegar*
- *2 vine ripened tomatoes*

Cook asparagus under a grill for 5 minutes or until tender. Serve drizzled with combined oil, vinegar and tomato.

Optional: For extra taste, sprinkle with 2 tbs. finely chopped basil leaves.

Bacon Stuffed Mushrooms

Serves 4

- *4 large organic field mushrooms*
- *4 rashers bacon*
- *½ cup breadcrumbs*
- *¾ cup mozzarella cheese*

Preheat oven to 180C. Remove mushroom stalks. Cut bacon rashers into fine strips and lightly fry. Mix breadcrumbs and cheese together and add bacon. Place mushrooms, top side down, on a lined baking tray. Spoon ingredients onto the mushroom and bake for 15 minutes.

Baked Sweet Pumpkin

Serves 4

- *1 small butternut pumpkin*
- *1 tsp. brown sugar*
- *½ tsp. butter*
- *2 tsp. ground cinnamon*

Preheat oven 190C. Cut off top of the pumpkin and scrape out all the seeds. Combine butter and brown sugar and spoon mixture into the pumpkin. Sprinkle with cinnamon and put the pumpkin lid back on. Sit pumpkin in a baking pan with 2cm of water in the bottom. Bake for 30 minutes, or until tender.

Baked Rice

Serves 4

- *1 cup rice, uncooked*
- *2 tbs. butter, melted*
- *500ml carton beef stock*
- *1/3 cup parmesan cheesed, shredded*

Preheat oven 180C. Place butter in a casserole dish, add rice and pour beef stock over rice. Sprinkle with parmesan and bake for 45 minutes.

Beans with Garlic & Pine Nuts

Serves 4. *These are scrumptious!*

- *400g beans*
- *3 tbs. olive oil*
- *1 or 2 cloves garlic, halved*
- *4 tbs. pine nuts*

Trim the beans, microwave for 1 minute then drain. Heat oil and garlic in small frying pan over low heat until garlic just changes colour. Add beans, sauté for a minute then add pine nuts that have been lightly toasted (on a baking tray in 180C oven for 3 minutes), stir until heated through.

Boiled Rice

Serves 4-6

- *2 cups water*
- *1 cup brown medium grain rice*

Bring water and rice to boil, stirring occasionally. Lower heat, cover and simmer for 15-20 minutes. Remove from heat and stand, covered, for a further 5 minutes. Rinse under hot water and serve.

Optional: Buy the Sun Rice 'Brown Rice in 90 seconds' microwave bags of rice from the supermarket...Even easier!

Caramelised Roast Pumpkin

Serves 4

- *½ kg butternut pumpkin*
- *3 tbs. olive oil*

Preheat oven 250C. Leave the skin on the pumpkin or if preferred, remove, discard the seeds and cut the flesh into chunks. Put the oil in a roasting pan and place on a medium heat. When simmering hot, add the pumpkin chunks and season generously with sea salt and pepper. Turn the pumpkin and allow to colour. Place the pan in the oven and roast for 30 - 35 minutes, turning occasionally until pumpkin has a crisp brown surface. Serve immediately or use in salads.

Cheesy Peas

Serves 4

- *500g frozen peas*
- *2.5 tbs. butter*
- *1 tbs. lemon juice*
- *1/3 cup parmesan cheese, shredded*

Microwave peas, butter and lemon juice on high for 3 minutes. Remove, stir and microwave for a further 2 minutes. Allow to stand covered for 2-3 minutes, transfer to serving dish and sprinkle with parmesan. Serve hot.

Crunchy Snow Peas

Serves 4. Thanks Michelle Dodd, for this terrific little tip!

- *400g snow peas*

Top and tail snow peas & place in a sealable container. Boil your jug, cover peas with boiling water and seal container for 3 minutes, drain and serve.

Easy Fried Rice

Serves 2. S.c.r.u.m.p.t.i.o.u.s

- *1 cup brown rice*
- *1 egg*
- *2 rashers bacon*
- *4 tbs. soy sauce*

While rice is boiling, fry the egg, breaking the yolk to ensure spreading. Dice bacon and fry until crisp. Drain rice and rinse under hot water, stirring it to separate. Drain thoroughly and add to bacon and egg, cover evenly with soy sauce.

Optional: Also nice with diced capsicum, pineapple, peas, chopped shallots & corn and a tsp. or 2 of sweet chilli sauce.

Fluffy Rice Without a Cooker

Serves 4-6. Recipe from Cyndi O'Meara.

- *5 cups boiling filtered water*
- *2.5 cups of long grain white rice, washed*

Preheat oven to 190C. Place rice in a large glass ovenproof casserole dish with a lid. Add boiling water and stir until lump free. Cover and cook in oven for 30 minutes.

Fried Brussels Sprouts

Serves 4

- *12 Brussels sprouts*
- *4 rashers bacon*
- *1 tbs. hazelnut oil*

Cut a criss-cross into the base of the sprouts. Boil approximately 8 minutes or until cooked. Dice bacon and then fry until crisp, fold through the cooked sprouts with hazelnut oil.

Garlic Mushrooms

Serves 4

- *500g mushrooms*
- *2 tbs. olive oil*
- *1 or 2 cloves garlic, crushed*
- *¼ cup fresh flat-leaf parsley*

Preheat oven 180C. Place mushrooms in a large baking dish, drizzle with oil and garlic, roast in oven 15 minutes or until mushrooms are tender and browned lightly. Stir in parsley.

Tip: Cook close to serving.

Honey Carrots

Serves 4-6

- *1 bunch baby carrots*
- *½ cup of water*
- *1 tbs. manuka honey*
- *2 tsp. butter*

Boil water in a saucepan. Place the carrots in water and return to the boil, simmer for 10 minutes. Drain, add honey and butter and toss well.

Honey Soy Noodles

Serves 4

- *500g pkt hokkien noodles*
- *1 tbs. macadamia oil*
- *2 tbs. tamari soy sauce*
- *2 tbs. manuka honey*

Soften noodles in a bowl filled with hot water, drain and set aside. Combine oil, soy sauce and honey together. Heat a wok to medium temperature and add oil, soy and honey mixture, quickly add noodles and stir continuously for about 3 minutes.

Optional: This dish is delicious with some cubed and stir fried chicken and a variety of vegetables.

Lemon Broccoli

Serves 4-6. Recipe from Cyndi O'Meara.

- *1 tbs. lemon juice fresh*
- *1 head broccoli cut into medium sized florets*

Bring 1 cup filtered water to the boil in a medium saucepan. Add broccoli, return to the boil and simmer for 3 minutes. Remove from heat and drain. Drizzle with lemon juice before serving.

Minted Pea Mash

Serves 4. Great with steak.

- *500g pontiac potatoes peeled and chopped*
- *3 cups frozen peas*
- *1/3 cup skim milk*
- *1/3 cup mint leaves chopped*

Cook potatoes in a large saucepan of boiling water until soft. Add peas and cook for 5 minutes. Drain & cool slightly. Return peas and potatoes to pan, add milk and mash with a potato masher until almost smooth, mix through mint leaves. Season well with salt and pepper.

Oven Baked Tomatoes

Serves 3

- 3 vine ripened tomatoes
- 3 tsp. basil pesto
- 3 tbs. parmesan

Cut the tomatoes in half. Place in an ovenproof dish, cut side up. Season each with sea salt and pepper. Smooth pesto over each and top with parmesan. Bake in a preheated 200C oven for 20 minutes.

Queensland Battered Vegetables

Serves 2

- 1 cup plain organic flour
- 1 bottle 4X beer (or beer of choice)
- 4 cups extra virgin olive oil
- 2 cups vegetables
  (mushrooms, sweet potatoes, capsicum, zucchini, carrots, squash, whole beans, cauliflower, broccoli, parsnips, all cut into bite-sized pieces)

Combine flour and beer in a big bowl and mix to make a thick, creamy batter. Generously dip and coat all vegetables in batter. Heat oil in a medium size saucepan.Fry vegetables till batter is golden brown. Remove, drain and lay on a paper towel to absorb extra oil. Serve warm.

Roast Beetroot

- *1 bunch whole beetroot*

Wash the beets well and trim the leaves leaving about 2cm of stalk. Remove most of the root, but not all. Do not peel. Wrap well in foil and bake in 180C oven for 40 minutes or until tender. Unwrap and peel.

Optional: Serve with grilled salmon, black pepper and butter or horseradish cream ... mmmmm!

Roasted Corn with Parmesan & Cayenne

Serves 4

- *4 fresh cobs of corn*
- *2 tbs. whole egg mayonnaise*
- *2 tbs. parmesan, grated*
- *½ tsp. cayenne pepper*

Preheat oven 180C. Place the corn in its husks in the oven and roast for 20 minutes until the corn is soft when you press on it. To finish, peel the husks, remove the corn silk, and tie the husks in a knot so you can hold on to it like a handle. Char the corn on a hot grill, or under a grill, until the kernels are slightly blackened all around and start popping (about 6 minutes). Rub the corn with mayonnaise, sprinkle with parmesan and cayenne pepper, ensure well coated.

Optional: Serve with lime wedges.

Sautéed Asparagus

Serves 4

- *2 bunches asparagus*
- *4 tbs. extra virgin olive oil*

Heat heavy based fry pan, douse with olive oil. Reduce heat and sauté asparagus until cooked, season lightly with sea salt and pepper.

Seasoned Roasted Vegetables

Serves 2

- *1 cup cold pressed macadamia oil*
- *1.5 tsp. oregano powder*
- *3 cups of vegies of choice (whole mushrooms; diced sweet potatoes; capsicum cut into 4 with seeds removed; topped and tailed zucchini; carrots sliced down the middle and halved; squash sliced in half; whole beans, onions halved, etc.)*

Preheat oven to 180C. Place vegetables on a baking tray. Coat in the oil and bake until cooked. Remove from tray and add to serving plate. Combine 1 tsp. sea salt and oregano and sprinkle over warm roasted vegetables.

Snow Peas in Garlic Mint Butter

Serves 8

- *200g snow peas*
- *1.5 tbs. butter*
- *2 cloves garlic, crushed*
- *1 tsp. mint, chopped*

Top and tail snow peas. Melt butter in a frying pan and then add garlic and mint. Stir in peas, sauté until just tender.

Steamed Broccoli scattered with Pine Nuts

Serves 4

- *1-2 heads of broccoli*
- *1-2 tbs. butter*
- *4 tbs. pine nuts, toasted*

Separate florets of broccoli and steam until just tender and still bright green. Place into serving dish, dot with butter, scatter with pine nuts and black pepper the lot.

Stuffed Capsicum

Makes 6

- *500g premium mince*
- *6 capsicums*
- *1 medium onion*

Preheat oven to 150C. Scrape out capsicums. Cook the mince and onion season generously with pepper and a little sea salt. Spoon into capsicum. Bake for ½ an hour on a lined baking dish.

Zucchini Hash Browns

Makes 4

- *1 cup zucchini, grated*
- *2 tbs. cold pressed macadamia oil for frying*
- *2 eggs, beaten slightly*
- *Organic mixed seasoning to taste*

Heat oil in a heavy pan. Mix all ingredients together in a medium size bowl and gently drop 1 tbs. of mixture in hot oil. When brown on one side, turn over and cook on the other side. Stack on a plate and keep warm until the whole batch is cooked.

Optional: Top with sweet chilli sauce, sour cream or butter.

MAINS

These days most people lead incredibly busy lives. The daily juggling acts of home, family, career, school and relationships have become more demanding than ever. Naturally, this affects the amount of time and effort required for the challenge of meal preparation.

You don't have to cook fancy or complicated masterpieces to fuel your body effectively, nor do you have to spend hours slaving away in the kitchen to impress. We believe a successful meal comprises just 4 ingredients;

- *Great food*
- *Great company*
- *A great drop of wine*
- *And the 4 Ingredient Recipe Book!*

Use this book as a tool to create fast and fabulous meals to WOW your family and friends. Remember to use fresh food or substitute with organic or home-grown where possible, as they are loaded with all the great nutrients your body needs to live to its highest potential.

Best Wishes & Happy Cooking!

Rachael & Kim

Beef

The opinions expressed by the man of this house are not necessarily those of the management.

(Anonymous)

Beef Patties

Serves 4. A recipe from the delightful Rebecca Butler.

- *500g lean mince*
- *1 cup mashed potatoes*
- *¼ cup finely chopped onions*
- *3 tbs. extra virgin olive oil*

Mix mince, potatoes and onions in a bowl, season with sea salt and pepper. Once combined, roll into patties. Heat oil in frying pan and depending on thickness cook, turning occasionally, until a crusty brown exterior forms all over.

Optional: Serve with the best ever gravy and vegetables.

Beef Stir Fry

Serves 4

- *500g stir fry beef*
- *2/3 cup barbequed stir fry sauce*
- *2 tbs. sesame oil*
- *4-6 shallots*

Mix stir fry sauce and meat together; allow to stand for 15 minutes. Heat oil in a wok or frying pan. Stir-fry meat in batches for 1 minute, or until cooked on the outside and medium on the inside. Trim the shallots and cut into thin lengthwise strips. Quickly stir-fry in wok. Serve meat on top of a salad (even just shredded ice-berg lettuce is nice) and top with shallots and jus.

Optional: This is delicious using just plain BBQ sauce if you don't have BBQ stir fry sauce.

Beef Stock

A recipe from Jan Neale.

- *1 kg beef soup bones*
- *1 bouquet garni*
- *2 onions, chopped coarsely*
- *1 cup of mixed vegetables (carrot, celery, capsicum etc whatever is available)*

Place all ingredients in saucepan, cover with water and boil. Reduce heat and simmer until meat is falling off the bones. Strip bones and discard. For a clear broth, strain.

Optional: Retain meat and vegetables to use in a casserole or curry.

Beef Stroganoff

Serves 4. Another beauty from Jan Neale.

- *500g beef strips*
- *1 cup mushrooms, chopped*
- *1 pkt beef stroganoff seasoning*
- *250g lite sour cream*

Heat a non-stick frying pan and lightly fry beef strips.
Add mushrooms, sour cream and stroganoff mix, stir well.
Add water to achieve your required consistency.

Beef Wellington

Serves 6. A recipe from Wendy Beattie. *This is a divine dinner party main.*

- *2.5 sheets puff pastry*
- *1.25kg fillet beef*
- *250g pepper pate*
- *1 cup sliced mushrooms*

Remove all fat from meat. Tie securely with string to hold shape. Grind black pepper over meat and press firmly. Heat a non-stick frying pan and sear meat until golden on all sides. Place meat on baking tray and put in 180C oven for 10 minutes. Remove and allow to become completely cold. Remove string. Beat pate until soft and spread a thin layer over meat. Sprinkle a little sea salt. Press thinly sliced mushrooms on top of meat. Wrap fillet in puff pastry, making sure it is totally concealed. Decorate top with strips of pastry and bake in a 250C oven for 5 minutes. Reduce heat to 180C and bake for further 30 - 40 minutes.

Optional: Brush pastry with beaten egg for a really presentable finish.

Chilli Con Carne

Serves 4

- *500g lean mince*
- *1 pkt chilli con carne mix*
- *425g can tomatoes*
- *310g can red kidney beans*

Brown mince in non-stick frying pan. Add chilli con carne mix. Add tomatoes, red kidney beans and ½ cup of water and stir well. Cover and simmer gently for 15 minutes, or until mince is cooked, stirring regularly.

Optional: We often add whatever other vegetables we have in the fridge; onions, carrots, capsicum, etc.

Coffee & Pepper Crusted Steaks

Serves 4. This is charmingly unusual!

- *4 steaks 2-3cm thick*
- *2 tbs. whole coffee beans*
- *2 tbs. whole black peppercorns*
- *Light olive oil for brushing or spraying steaks*

Coarsely grind the coffee beans and peppercorns. Press the mixture evenly on both sides of the steaks. Brush or spray steaks lightly with oil, then grill or barbecue the steaks over direct high heat for 8 to 10 minutes, turning once halfway through grilling time (do not turn steaks until you see beads of juice on the surface). Remove the steaks from the grill and season both sides with sea salt. Allow to rest for 2 to 3 minutes before serving.

Creamy Meatballs

Serves 4-6

- *750g of extra lean mince*
- *250g lite sour cream*
- *1 tsp. sea salt*
- *1 tsp. garlic powder*

Combine all except half the sour cream. Using a generous tablespoon, roll into balls. Brown in a frying pan and place in a casserole dish. Dilute remaining sour cream with 2 tbs. water mix well then spread over the meatballs and bake at 160C for 30 minutes.

Easy Roast Beef

Serves 4-6. A recipe from Shane McCosker.
This is a sensational Sunday roast and sooooooooo easy!

- *1 kg beef rib roast*
- *1 pkt French onion soup mix*
- *420g can cream of mushroom soup*

Preheat oven to 180C. Place a large sheet of alfoil in frying pan, enough to fully wrap the beef. Place beef in the centre of the foil and bring foil up to make a bowl. Combine soups in a bowl. Mix thoroughly and spread over beef roast. Fold alfoil to seal tightly. Bake 1 hour or until tender, serve with delicious gravy in the bottom of the bag.

Optional: Serve with roast vegetables.

Glen's Corned Beef

Serves 6. A recipe perfected by Glen, Kim's husband.

- *1 kg corned beef*
- *1.25 litres of ginger ale*

Place meat in large pot, add the ginger ale and cook for 1 hour or until tender.

Optional: Serve with vegetables and horseradish sauce.

Kim's Corned Beef

Serves 6.

- *1 kg corned beef*
- *6 cloves*
- *1/3 cup maple syrup*
- *Black pepper*

Place meat in a large pot, cover with water. Bring to boil, reduce heat and cook for 1 hour or until tender. When cooked, place meat in a shallow baking dish, press cloves into meat, drizzle with syrup and dust with freshly cracked pepper. Place in preheated 180C oven to glaze for 15 minutes.

Pan-Fried Steak

Serves 2. Mouth-watering!

- *2 x 200g eye fillet steaks*
- *2 tbs. extra virgin olive oil*

Preheat heavy frying pan until the pan is hot. Add oil and reduce heat by a quarter. Place steak in pan and cook for 10 minutes for medium doneness (season with sea salt and pepper ½ way through this), turn once only, then cook until desired doneness is achieved. Take eye fillet off heat and let it rest for 5-10 minutes.

Pesto Stuffed Steaks

Serves 4. F.a.s.t & F.a.b.u.l.o.u.s

- *2 beef rib eye steaks (about 3cm thick)*
- *¼ cup basil pesto*
- *3 tbs. parmesan cheese, shaved*
- *1 tbs. extra virgin olive oil*

Preheat heavy frying pan until the pan is hot.   Cut into the side of each steak, forming a deep pocket (do not cut through). Mix pesto and cheese and spread into pockets. Press closed and drizzle oil over beef. Place steaks carefully in the pan and cook for 10 minutes for medium doneness; turn once when you see juices on the surface of the steak. When done, remove, cover and let stand for 5-10 minutes. Cut beef into thick strips to serve.

Quick Meatloaf

Serves 4

- *500g premium organic mince*
- *3 free range eggs, lightly beaten*
- *¾ cup of organic breadcrumbs*
- *4.5 tbs. tomato paste – reserve an extra tablespoon*

Preheat oven to 180C. Mix all ingredients together and place in a lined rectangular baking dish. Spread reserved tomato paste on top of meatloaf. Bake for 50 minutes or until lightly browned on top. Serve hot with vegetables, salad or mash potato. This is also great to freeze.

Optional: For an added zing add 1 tsp. of curry powder. To get your 5 vegetable quota for the day, add shredded carrot, sweet potato, diced mushrooms, and peas and corn to the mix before baking.

Rissoles

Makes 8. From playgroup chef extraordinaire, Aine Watkins!

- *500g premium mince*
- *2 medium onions*
- *2 medium eggs*
- *1 lbs./flour*

Preheat a sandwich press machine. Mix all ingredients, except for flour. Divide into 8 even amounts and roll into balls, binding with a small amount of flour. Place in between the sandwich press plates and cook till done.

Roast Beef with Horseradish Cream

Serves 4

- *1kg beef rib roast*
- *1 tbs. mixed sea salt and pepper*
- *½ tsp. dried thyme*
- *Horseradish cream*

Heat oven to 150C. Rub the roast with salt, pepper and thyme. Arrange roast in large shallow roasting pan. Roast about 2 hours 15 minutes in the lower third of your oven. Transfer roast to a carving board and cover loosely with alfoil. Let stand 15 minutes. Carve and serve with horseradish cream.

Salsa Patties

Serves 4-6. A recipe from the beautiful Rebecca Butler.

- *750g lean mince*
- *1/3 cup salsa*
- *1/3 savoury biscuits, finely crushed*
- *2 tbs. olive oil*

Combine, mince, salsa and biscuits. Roll into 6 patties. Heat frying pan, add oil and brown patties.

Optional: Delicious served with rice, salad and a dollop of quacamole.

Veal Casserole

Serves 4. This is a third generation Kellow family secret (that's not much of a secret anymore) … Thanks for sharing, Jocelyn and Juleen, as this is too easy and too tasty!

- *500g diced veal*
- *200g diced bacon*
- *1 cup sliced celery*
- *420g can cream of chicken soup*

Pour all ingredients into a casserole dish. Place in a moderate oven and bake at 160C for 2 hours.

Veal Marsala

Serves 4.

- *500g veal steak*
- *3 tbs. butter*
- *½ cup marsala*
- *¼ cup plain flour*

Pound veal with a mallet to flatten. Season flour with sea salt and pepper and dust veal. Heat a frypan, add butter to melt. Add veal and cook 2 minutes on each side. Add marsala and cook a further 3-4 minutes to form a sauce with pan juices.

Chicken

"The more we share, the more we have"

Anonymous

Apricot Chicken

Serves 4

- *8 chicken pieces*
- *500g can apricot nectar*
- *1 pkt French onion soup*
- *1 brown onion, diced*

Place chicken pieces in a casserole dish with soup and onion and season with sea salt and pepper. Add apricot nectar and stir. Cover and bake in 180C oven for 1.5 hrs.

Optional: For a change, place chicken in a plastic bag and coat in flour, salt and pepper and lightly fry. Cook then for only 1 hr in oven.

Cajun Chicken Kebabs

Serves 1. Light and luscious with a simple salad!

- *140g chicken breast fillet, cubed*
- *½ red capsicum*
- *½ brown onion*
- *2 tsp. cajun seasoning*

Preheat grill on high. Thread cubes of chicken, capsicum and onion onto skewers (soak in water first). Sprinkle with seasoning then, grill for 2 minutes each side, or until cooked through.

Cheese & Prosciutto Chicken

Serves 4. Another great recipe from Wendy Beattie's vibrant kitchen.

- *4 chicken fillet breasts*
- *4 slices Swiss cheese*
- *8 slices prosciutto*
- *2 tbs. extra virgin olive oil*

Preheat oven 200C. Cut lengthways through each fillet to make a pocket, leaving 1 cm at each end. Fill each fillet with cheese and prosciutto. Heat oil in large frying pan over med/high heat. Add chicken breasts and cook for 1 - 2 minutes until golden on each side. Transfer to baking tray and roast for 7 - 10 minutes, or until just cooked through. Cover and set aside to rest for 5 minutes.

Optional: Serve with sweet potato mash and baby spinach.

Chicken & Jarlsberg Casserole

Serves 6. A recipe by Julie McDonald OAM
www.juliemcdonald.org

- *6 chicken fillet breasts*
- *6 slices jarlsberg cheese*
- *420g can cream of chicken soup*
- *¼ cup milk*

Preheat oven 180C. Place chicken in a casserole dish and cover with cheese. Mix well soup and milk and pour over chicken. Bake for an hour at 150C.

Chicken Pie

- *2 sheets puff pastry*
- *440g can condensed cream of chicken soup*
- *1 cup cooked chicken without skin, cubed*
- *500g frozen mixed vegies, thawed*

Preheat oven to 180C. Line a greased pie dish with the first sheet of puff pastry. Combine remaining ingredients in a bowl, season with salt and pepper and pour into pastry. Cover with remaining sheet, seal edges well by pressing with a fork. Cut several slits in the pie lid and bake for 30 minutes, or until lid is golden brown.

Optional: Brush with beaten egg or milk for a very presentable finish.

Chicken, Pumpkin & Chickpea Curry

Serves 6

- *700g piece pumpkin*
- *8 boneless, skinless chicken thighs*
- *300g can chickpeas*
- *435g jar korma curry sauce*

De-seed pumpkin, wrap in cling film and microwave on high for 5 minutes or until almost cooked. Peel and cut into cubes. Cut chicken thighs in half. Drain chickpeas. Place chicken, pumpkin, chickpeas and curry sauce in a saucepan. Wash jar with about ¼ cup of hot water and add to saucepan. Cover and cook on medium for about 30 minutes.

Optional: Serve with steamed rice and garnish with fresh coriander.

Chicken Stir Fry

Serves 2. This is effortless!!

- *300g chicken breast fillets, sliced*
- *3 tbs. sweet chilli sauce*
- *3 tbs. hoisin sauce*
- *3 tbs. soy sauce*

Slice the chicken breast fillets into thin slices. Line electric frying pan with baking paper and heat on high. Add sweet chilli, hoisin and soy sauce and stir well. When the sauce begins to bubble, add the chicken fillets and stir to combine. Cook until the chicken is done (approximately 5 minutes).

Optional: Add whatever vegetables available, sauté and serve with rice.

Chicken Schnitzel

Serves 4. A family favourite!

- *4 chicken schnitzels*
- *4 tbs. extra virgin olive oil*
- *1 cup napolitane sauce*
- *1 cup mozzarella cheese*

Heat frying pan and add oil. When hot, lightly fry chicken schnitzels. When golden brown on both sides, place on alfoil on a baking tray. Top evenly with napolitane sauce and mozzarella cheese and grill slowly until cheese is bubbling and golden.

Chutney Chicken Dish

Serves 2. This is deliciously simple!

- *2 chicken breasts*
- *2 tbs. rosella fruit chutney*
- *2 tbs. French mustard*
- *¼ cup cheddar cheese, grated*

Mix the chutney with the mustard and cover the chicken breasts. Put chicken breasts in a baking dish, cover with grated cheese and place in oven for 15-20 minutes at 180C.

Optional: Serve with rice or vegetables.

Green Chicken Curry

Serves 4. A ripper recipe from Shane McCosker.

- *4 chicken thighs, boneless and skinless*
- *1 cup green beans, cut into 5 cm pieces*
- *¼ cup green curry paste*
- *400 ml can coconut cream*

Cut chicken into strips. Heat your wok or large frying pan; add green curry paste, cooking and stirring for a minute or so or until fragrant. Add chicken and cook, stirring for about 10 minutes, until almost done. Stir in coconut cream and bring to boil. Simmer uncovered for 30 minutes. Add beans and simmer for 10 minutes, or until just tender.

Optional: We often add more vegetables.

Grilled Chicken with Roasted Capsicum & Tomato Sauce

Serves 4

- *4 red capsicums*
- *8 skinless chicken drumsticks*
- *¼ cup sun-dried tomato pesto*
- *1 large tomato*

Cut capsicums in half, de-seed and place cut side down under grill. Place chicken under grill also and grill until capsicum skin starts to blister. Remove capsicum and continue to cook chicken until juices run clear, 15-20 minutes. Remove skin and blend with pesto until smooth. Cut tomato in half, de-seed and chop into small cubes. Serve chicken with roasted capsicum and tomato sauce, topped with cubed tomato.

Honey Baked Chicken

Serves 4-6

- *1 pkt French onion soup*
- *¾ cup white wine or water*
- *3 tbs. honey*
- *1 kg chicken pieces*

Combine French onion soup, honey and white wine and pour evenly over chicken pieces in a shallow ovenproof dish. Cover and bake at 160C for 1 hour, remove cover and bake uncovered for 30 minutes.

Honey Mustard Chicken Breasts

Serves 4

- *4 chicken breast fillets*
- *¼ cup honey*
- *2 tbs. dijon mustard*

Pound the chicken breast fillets. Mix the honey and mustard and spread over the chicken leaving a little for basting. Grill for 15 to 20 minutes, turning and basting until done.

Kazza's Wonderful Chicken

Serves 2.   A recipe from Karyn Turnbull-Markus.

- *2 chicken breast fillets*
- *½ cup lite sour cream*
- *¼ cup slithered almonds*
- *½ cup grated jarslberg cheese*

Dip breasts into sour cream, mix almonds & jarslberg together and then roll chicken in this – coat well. Place in shallow oven dish & bake at 160C for about 20 minutes, or until chicken is golden brown.

Mascarpone & Coriander Chicken

Serves 4. A super recipe from Janelle McCosker.

- *6 chicken thigh fillets*
- *4 tbs. mascarpone*
- *½ cup coriander, chopped*
- *1 tbs. extra virgin olive oil*

Quarter each chicken thigh. Heat oil in a frying pan, add chicken and cook until golden, turning occasionally. Add mascarpone and stir until melted, simmer and allow to bubble. Add coriander and mix well, remove from heat and season with sea salt and pepper.

Pesto & Chicken Parcels

Serves 4. A recipe from the extremely energetic Kelly Mauger.

- *4 chicken thighs*
- *4 tbs. basil pesto*
- *125g camembert cheese*
- *2 sheets puffed pastry*

Preheat oven 180C. Rub one side of the chicken thigh with pesto and season with sea salt and pepper. Cut camembert into thin strips and cover chicken. Start from one end of the chicken thigh and roll it up. Place a sheet of the puffed pastry flat and cut diagonally, place the chicken in the middle and fold to cover sealing the edges with a fork. Bake for 30 minutes.

Polynesian Chicken

Serves 4

- *500g can crushed pineapple, drained*
- *4 chicken breasts*
- *250g jar peach or apricot preserves*
- *Macadamia nut oil cooking spray*

Preheat oven 190C. Arrange chicken breasts in an ovenproof dish. Spray with macadamia oil and bake uncovered for 30 minutes. Turn chicken over and bake for an additional 15 minutes or until tender. Drain off pan juices. Mix pineapple and peach/apricot preserves together. Pour over chicken and bake for another 15 minutes, or until hot and bubbly.

Sweet & Spicy Chicken

Serves 2

- *6 chicken legs*
- *½ cup orange marmalade*
- *1-2 tsp. chilli powder*

Preheat oven to 180C. Combine marmalade and chilli powder in a plastic sandwich bag, add chicken legs and shake until evenly coated. Place chicken on alfoil on a baking tray and spoon on any remaining marmalade/chilli powder. Bake for 30 minutes or until done.

Tomato Flavoured Chicken Legs

Serves 4-6. A recipe from Verna Day.

- *1 kg chicken legs*
- *420g can tomato soup*
- *1 pkt French onion soup*

Preheat oven to 180C. Place chicken legs in an ovenproof dish. Combine tomato soup, French onion mix and ½ cup water then pour over chicken legs. Bake for 1 hour.

Zingy Chicken

Serves 4

- *4 chicken breasts*
- *1 egg, beaten*
- *¼ cup soya sauce*
- *1 cup of crushed cornflakes*

Cut chicken into thickish strips. Combine egg and soya sauce and dip chicken pieces into it. Coat with crushed cornflakes, place on a baking sheet on a baking tray and cook at 180C for 30-40 minutes.

Fish

Great love and great achievements involve great risks!

Anonymous

Baked Fish

Serves 2

- *2 fresh white fish fillets*
- *1 tsp. butter*
- *1 lemon*

Coat fish with melted butter and then season with salt and pepper. Cut lemon and put slices on fish. Wrap fish in alfoil. Cook in 180C oven for 20 minutes or until fish is tender.

Baked Salmon with Pesto Crust

Serves 4. A recipe from the talented Michelle Dodd.
THIS IS FANTASTIC!

- *4 salmon steaks*
- *1 jar basil pesto*
- *½ cup pecorino cheese, finely grated*
- *1 lemon*

Sear salmon steaks on each side for 2 minutes, skin side down first. Meanwhile combine pesto and cheese. Spread this mixture over salmon steaks and squeeze fresh lemon juice over the top. Bake in a moderate oven for 15 minutes.

Caesar's Fish

Serves 2

- *2 fresh white fish fillets*
- *½ cup caesar salad dressing*
- *1 cup crushed cornflakes*
- *½ cup shredded cheddar cheese*

Preheat oven 160C. Arrange fillets in a single layer on a lined baking dish. Drizzle fillets with dressing. Sprinkle cornflakes over the top. Bake for 10 minutes. Top with cheese and bake for an additional 5 minutes, or until fish easily flakes with a fork.

Creamy Basil Fish

Serves 4

- *4 fresh white fish fillets*
- *3 tbs. fresh basil leaves, finely chopped*
- *1 tbs. lemon juice*
- *4 tbs. lite sour cream*

Grill fish under a hot grill for about 3 minutes each side, until cooked. Place basil, juice and cream in a small saucepan and heat slowly – do not boil. Serve over fish.

Optional: This is magic served with sautéed lemon potatoes and salad.

Curried Fish with Coconut Rice

Serves 4. This is a great way to make rice for a change!

- *4 fresh white fish fillets*
- *283g jar Korma curry sauce*
- *400g can coconut milk*
- *1 cup jasmine rice*

Cut fish into 2cm cubes. Place in a saucepan with curry sauce.
Bring to the boil and simmer for 5 minutes or until fish is cooked.
Bring ½ cup water and coconut milk to the boil. Add rice and cook
for 12-15 minutes or until rice is tender and liquid absorbed. Pile
rice onto four individual serving plates. Top with fish mixture.

Optional: Garnish with fresh coriander.

Dill Prawns

Serves 4

- *4 cloves garlic*
- *500g cooked king prawns, peeled and de-veined*
- *2 tbs. butter*
- *½ tsp. dried dill*

In a small frying pan, melt butter. Add garlic and cook over low heat
until garlic begins to turn light brown. Discard garlic and add dill.
Next, add prawns, cook and stir over medium heat for about 3-4
minutes. Serve over rice.

Filo Fish

Serves 4. This is so versatile.

- *8 sheets filo pastry*
- *4 fillets fresh boneless fish*
- *2.5 cups tomato sauce*
- *2 tbs. extra virgin olive oil*

Preheat oven 200C. Brush a sheet of filo pastry with some olive oil and lay a second sheet on top. Place a piece of fish (or chicken) at the bottom of the pastry and spoon on some tomato sauce (or a couple of slices of mango and some cheese) and roll over tucking in pastry sides to make a neat and closed pastry parcel. Lay parcels on a baking paper lined tray and brush the top of each with some more olive oil before baking for 12 minutes or until golden brown.

Optional: If you're all fished out, try replacing the fish and tomato sauce with chicken, mango and cheese – yum!

Fish Fillets with Orange Sauce

Serves 4

- *4 fresh white fish fillets*
- *1 orange*
- *2 tbs. dry white wine*
- *3 tbs. butter*

Place 1 tbs. butter in heavy frying pan and heat. Place fish in pan. Blend 2 tbs. orange juice and wine with remaining 2 tbs. melted butter; pour half over the fish fillets. Sprinkle with sea salt, pepper and 2 tbs. orange zest. Cook for 2 minutes; pour remaining sauce over fish and continue cooking until fish is done. Fish should flake easily with a fork.

Fish with Black Bean Sauce

Serves 4

- *4 tbs. black bean and garlic sauce*
- *1 tbs. sesame oil*
- *4 fish steaks*
- *4 tbs. sesame seeds*

Mix black bean and garlic sauce and sesame oil together. Spread on fish steaks. Sprinkle with sesame seeds and grill for 4 minutes each side, or until fish is cooked.

Garlic Cream King Prawns

Serves 4. A classic from Aine Watkins that'll make anyone a Chef!

- *16 cooked king or tiger prawns, peeled or de-veined*
- *½ cup of cream*
- *1 tbs. freshly crushed garlic*
- *2 cups of rice*

Boil rice, then rinse under hot water. Meanwhile, place garlic and cream in a wok or fry pan and reduce. Add prawns till heated and serve on a bed of rice.

Ginger Prawns

Serves 4

- *1 clove garlic*
- *500g cooked prawns, peeled and de-veined*
- *2 tsp. minced ginger*
- *2 tbs. lemon juice*

Crush, peel and finely chop garlic. Sauté garlic and ginger in a non-stick pan for 2 minutes. Mix in lemon juice and prawns and cook on low for 5 more minutes. Serve immediately.

Grilled Fish with Tomato Pickle Dressing

Serves 4

- *4 fresh white fish fillets*
- *2 tbs. drained capers*
- *Tomato pickle dressing*

Grill fish until golden brown. Top with tomato pickle dressing and sprinkle capers over.

Optional: Delicious served with sautéed lemon potatoes and salad.

Herbed Barramundi

Serves 2

- *2 fresh barramundi fillets*
- *2 tbs. fresh flat-leaf parsley, chopped*
- *2 tbs. fresh basil leaves, chopped*
- *2 tbs. fresh lemon juice*

Char-grill barramundi for 3 minutes each side. Top with herbs and lemon juice and serve with roast vegetables ... *Yummy!!*

Lemon Grilled Fish

Serves 4

- *4 fresh white fish fillets*
- *1 tbs. lemon pepper seasoning*
- *1 whole shallot, finely chopped*

Sprinkle fish generously with lemon pepper seasoning. Cover and refrigerate for 15 minutes. Cook fish under a preheated grill or barbecue until flesh is white and flakes easily when tested with a fork. Garnish with shallots.

Moroccan Salmon

Serves 2. This is divine; everyone that we have served this to has requested the recipe!!

- *2 salmon steaks*
- *Macadamia nut oil spray*
- *Moroccan seasoning*

Place salmon on alfoil on a baking tray. Spray with cooking oil and coat thoroughly with Moroccan seasoning. Bake at 160C for 15 minutes or to your liking.

A sensational salad to match

Warm corn salad, it is toooooooo easy and soooooooo
yummy, although more than 4 ingredients,
we just had to add it!

- *2 cob corn (cook in the microwave for 10 minutes)*
- *1 avocado, cubed*
- *1 tomato and ½ Spanish onion, diced*
- *Juice from ½ -1 lemon*
- *4 tbs. fresh coriander, roughly chopped*

Mix altogether and place Moroccan salmon on top.
A GREAT ENTERTAINER!!

Pan-Fried Fish

Serves 4

- *4 fresh white fish fillets*
- *3-4 slices of stale bread, finely grated*
- *1 egg, beaten*
- *3 tbs. extra virgin olive oil*

Season bread generously with sea salt and pepper. Dip fillets into
egg and then into breadcrumbs. Heat a heavy based frying pan,
doused with olive oil. Cook the fish on both sides for 3 minutes, or
until cooked to your liking; remove from heat and allow to rest.

Salmon & Spinach Filo

Serves 2

- *2 salmon steaks (without the skin)*
- *¾ - 1 cup frozen spinach, thawed, excess liquid squeezed out*
- *4 sheets filo pastry*
- *Macadamia nut oil spray*

Preheat oven 180C. Place spinach in a bowl and season with sea salt and pepper. Place 2 sheets of filo on a flat surface and spray with oil, place other two on top. Place salmon in centre of each and top with spinach. Spray with oil and fold pastry to enclose salmon. Spray with oil and place on a baking tray. Bake for 25 minutes or until golden and cooked.

Optional: Crush a clove of garlic into the spinach for an enriching flavour. This is nice served with Horseradish cream.

Tony's Delicious Quick Mango Fish

Serves 4. A recipe by the adorable Tony Van Dijk.

- *4 pieces of fresh fish, boned and cleaned (swordfish/mahi mahi or marlin)*
- *½ cup extra virgin olive oil*
- *2 fresh mangoes*
- *Cracked pepper*

Coat fish liberally with extra virgin olive oil and cracked pepper. Cook on a medium heated BBQ surface or flat fry pan. Cook fish till you can see the flesh turning white up to half way through, and then grind some more cracked pepper onto the exposed non-cooked surface before flipping over. Serve with BBQ or pan-cooked fresh mango flesh.

Lamb

Always borrow money from a pessimist.
He won't expect it back.

Asian Style Lamb Cutlets

Serves 4

- *10 lamb cutlets*
- *1/3 cup dry sherry*
- *1/3 cup soy sauce*

Trim fat from cutlets. Marinate cutlets in sherry and soy sauce for 10 minutes. Drain and reserve marinade. Heat grill on high. Grill cutlets each side, brushing occasionally with marinade.

Lamb & Bacon Parcels

Serves 4

- *4 loin lamb chops*
- *2 rashers of bacon, cut in half*
- *4 tbs. wholegrain mustard*
- *2 sheets puff pastry*

Cut the meat from the bone and trim off fat. Cut the puff pastry sheets in half and spread each generously with mustard. Place the lamb in the middle of the pastry and top with a half rasher of bacon. Seal edges and bake in 180C oven for 20-30 minutes or until golden brown.

Optional: For a presentable finish, baste the pastry with a beaten egg. Can substitute mustard with basil pesto for a change

---

Lamb Shank Casserole

Serves 4

- *4 lamb shanks*
- *1 large onion, coarsely chopped*
- *1 pkt French onion soup*
- *1 tsp. worcestershire sauce*

Place lamb shanks and onions into a large saucepan. Mix soup and sauce together with about 3 cups of water and pour over shanks. Cook on low for 4 hours and serve over mashed potato.

Optional: Add 2 tbs. of tomato sauce, for flavour. Add 1 cup of mixed vegetables that you may have e.g. carrot, celery, broccoli, cauliflower, squash, brussel sprouts.

Oat Crusted Lamb Cutlets

Serves 4

- *800g lamb cutlets*
- *1 cup small oats*
- *4 tbs. parmesan cheese*
- *2 eggs*

Preheat oven 190C. For best result put oats through food processor or blender, then combine them with parmesan cheese. Dip cutlets in beaten egg, then oat mixture to coat. Place on alfoil in a baking tray. Bake for 30 minutes or until golden brown.

Optional: Add 1 tbs. mixed herbs to the oats and parmesan for added flavour.

Roast Lamb

Makes 4-6. A recipe by Jan Neale. *One we love to be invited to on a Sunday night.*

- *1kg leg of lamb (or shoulder)*
- *1 sprig rosemary*
- *2 cloves garlic, sliced*
- *2 tbs. olive oil*

Cut a 2 cm slit across the lamb in several places and insert 6 rosemary leaves and a slice of garlic. Coat the baking dish with oil and bake in a 200C oven for about 1 hour. Serve with roast vegetables and best gravy ever.

Tandoori Lamb

Makes 4-5. A recipe from our treasured Anthony 'Spud' Moore.

- *8 lamb cutlets*
- *1 cup tandoori paste*
- *1 cup natural yoghurt*
- *¼ cup coriander, chopped*

Trim lamb cutlets of unwanted fat. Mix tandoori paste, half the yoghurt and half the coriander and coat lamb. Allow to stand in a covered bowl for 1 hour in the fridge. Pan-fry cutlets until ¾ cooked. Drizzle remaining yoghurt and tandoori over the top of the cooking cutlets and finally sprinkle with the remaining coriander...mmmmm!

Tangy Lamb Balls

Serves 4. A recipe from Perditta O'Connor worth trying!

- *500g lamb mince*
- *1 tsp. curry powder*
- *3 tbs. sweet chilli sauce*
- *Juice of 1 lemon*

Place all ingredients into a large bowl and combine. Roll into patties and fry in a non-stick frying pan until crunchy on the outside (this means it is cooked well on the inside).

Optional: Add a clove of garlic to the mixture. Serve with jasmine rice and a mint yoghurt dipping sauce. Roll into small balls and serve with sweet chilli sauce as a nibble on their own.

Pasta

'Al dente' is used to describe when pasta is cooked to perfection. 'Al dente' in Italian literally means "to the tooth". Pasta that is al dente should not be overly firm, nor should it be overly soft

...Good luck!!!

AB's Pasta

Serves 4. A recipe by Alistair Beattie that shocked us with its simplicity and taste!

- *300g tubular spaghetti*
- *4 rashers rindless bacon, diced*
- *½ cup pine nuts*
- *190g jar sun-dried tomato pesto*

While you are cooking pasta, fry bacon until brown. Toast pine nuts for 2-3 minutes in preheated oven 150C. When spaghetti is ready, drain and rinse with boiling water. Mix with 4 tbs. of pesto and toss through bacon and pine nuts. Add more pesto, if required.

Easy Pasta

Serves 4

- *500g lean mince*
- *4 zucchinis, sliced*
- *4 cups spaghetti sauce*
- *350g fresh angel's hair pasta*

Heat a heavy frying pan over medium high heat. Sauté meat and zucchini in 3 tbs. of water for 5-6 minutes, stirring frequently to break up meat. Stir in spaghetti sauce and simmer until just heated through. Cook pasta in a large pan of boiling water for about 3 minutes. Drain, rinse with boiling water and place on plates topped with prepared sauce.

Optional: Sprinkle with parmesan cheese ... the kids will love it!

Florentine Carbonara

Serves 4. Recipe from Julie Stephens. *THIS IS TIMELESS!!*

- *2 eggs lightly beaten*
- *1.5 cups parmesan cheese, grated*
- *5 rashes rindless bacon diced*
- *350g spaghetti*

Bring a medium bowl of water to the boil. Add spaghetti and boil till al dente (around 8 minutes). While spaghetti is boiling, lightly fry bacon strips in a frying pan. Once spaghetti is cooked, drain and add beaten eggs immediately, stirring through hot pasta. Add bacon, sprinkle with cheese and serve.

Optional: Fry bacon with a little garlic.

Garden Penne Pasta

Serves 4

- *2 cups penne pasta*
- *1 cup fresh basil, chopped*
- *5 tomatoes, diced*
- *4 tbs. extra virgin olive oil*

Add pasta to a saucepan of boiling water, stir immediately and cook uncovered for 12 minutes or until al dente, stirring occasionally. Drain and add the remaining ingredients, lightly toss to combine.

Optional: Crack fresh ground pepper to taste.

Meg's Pasta

Serves 2. A recipe by Meg Wilson.

- *200g pasta*
- *100g prosciutto, shredded*
- *1 ripe avocado, cubed*
- *3tbs. chilli oil*

Bring water to the boil. Add pasta and cook until tender. Remove and drain, add remaining ingredients and serve.

Optional: Prosciutto can be replaced by 100g cooked prawns.

Pasta with Crab & Lemon Cream Sauce

Serves 4. A recipe from Kirsty Morrison.

- *500g spiral pasta*
- *300ml cream*
- *1 lemon*
- *400g freshly cooked crab meat*

Bring water to the boil. Add pasta and cook until tender. Meanwhile, finely grate the lemon rind then heat cream and rind in a medium sized saucepan; bring to boil. Add crabmeat and stir gently until heated through. Remove from heat and pour over pasta... yummmmmmmmmmmmmmm!!

Optional: This is really nice with ¼ cup of freshly chopped flat-leaf parsley mixed through it.

Quick Spaghetti

Serves 4. Recipe from Deb Harris.

- *1 pkt thin, organic spaghetti*
- *1 tbs. extra light olive oil*
- *Choice of bacon, sun dried tomatoes, sweet chilli sauce, prawns, mushrooms, and avocado.*

Bring water to the boil. Add spaghetti and cook for 8 minutes, or until al dente. Remove from heat, drain.   Add 1 tbs. of olive oil and extra ingredient (pre-cook ingredients such as bacon, prawns, mushrooms), toss through spaghetti.

Optional: Can serve with a little black pepper and sprinkled with parmesan cheese

Pork

"The difference between 'involvement' and 'commitment' is like an eggs and ham breakfast; the chicken was 'involved' - the pig was 'committed'."

Anonymous

Apricot & Mustard Pork Chops

Serves 4. Kim's father-in-law loves these!!

- *1/3 cup apricot jam*
- *2 tbs. dijon mustard*
- *4 pork loin chops*
- *3 shallots, finely chopped*

In a small saucepan over low heat, cook and stir apricot jam and mustard until jam is melted; set aside. Place pork chops under grill and grill for 3 minutes each side. Brush with half of the glaze and grill for another 3 minutes each side. Brush with the remaining glaze and grill a further 2-4 minutes or until meat juices run clear. Top with shallots. Serve over rice.

Chinese BBQ Pork Fillet

Serves 6. A recipe by Anthony 'Spud' Moore.
Simple & Scrumptious!!

- *1.5kg pork fillet*
- *1 pkt red pork seasoning**
- *400ml Char-Sui sauce (Chinese BBQ sauce)**
- *¼ cup fresh coriander*

Trim fat off pork and cut into four portions. Mix all ingredients together and wet with 1 cup of water. Coat the pork well and marinate overnight in the fridge. Cook on a grill, BBQ or fry pan.

* Can be bought at most big supermarkets or Asian food store.

Fried Sausages

Serves 4

- *8 sausages*
- *2 tbs. plain flour*
- *4 tbs. extra virgin olive oil*

Prick sausages with a fork, season flour with sea salt and pepper. Roll sausages in seasoned flour then gently fry in hot oil turning every 5 minutes for about 15-20 minutes or until browned.

Optional: Serve with best gravy ever and mashed potatoes.

Ham on the Bone

Serves 8. Another by Kendra Horwood. A Christmas Champion!

- ½ ham on the bone
- 150g ham glaze or a jar of marmalade
- 30 cloves
- 24 fresh, plump cherries

Preheat oven 170C. Remove outer skin of ham and reserve (use when storing ham to keep moist). Using a sharp knife, score the fat into diamond shapes and push cloves into the creases. Place ham on rack in a roasting tray and brush with glaze. Pour 1.25 cups of water into roasting pan. Bake ham for 25 minutes until golden, remove from oven and set aside. If there is liquid in the base of the pan, place on the stove and reduce over medium heat until syrupy. Pour over ham before serving. Garnish the ham with cherries before serving.

Pork & Bacon Wraps

Serves 4. D.E.L.I.C.I.O.U.S!

- 2 pork fillets
- 1/3 cup basil pesto
- 4 rashers rindless bacon
- ½ cup apple sauce

Cut pork fillets in half. Spread outside with 2/3 of basil pesto. Wrap bacon around fillets to cover outside. Bake in 180C oven for 25-30 minutes or until pork is cooked. Mix remaining pesto with apple sauce and heat until almost boiling, serve with fillets.

Pork Chop Casserole

Serves 4. A recipe from Margaret Tindale.

- *4 pork chops*
- *420g can cream of mushroom soup*
- *300g can peas*
- *¼ cup chopped onion*

Trim the pork chops of excess fat and place in casserole dish. Mix mushroom soup, peas and onion and pour over pork chops and cover with casserole lid. Bake in a preheated 150C oven for 45 minutes, remove lid, increase heat to 180C and bake a further 15 minutes or until cooked.

Optional: Serve with roast vegetables.

Pork Spare Ribs

Serves 4. These are SOOOO nice!!

- *8 pork spare ribs*
- *375g bottle honey, soy and garlic marinade*

Boil ribs first for 5-10 minutes to rid excess fat. Drain, place ribs on alfoil spread across a large baking tray. Cover both sides of each rib generously with marinade.   Place in the refrigerator for at least half an hour before cooking. Place under grill, cooking 5 minutes each side until juices run clear. Continue basting throughout.

Optional: Serve with rice and crunchy snow peas.

Pork Tenderloin Bake

Serves 6. Quick. Easy. Yummy … Gotta Love it!!

- *600g pork tenderloin*
- *420g can tomato soup*
- *1 pkt French onion soup*
- *2 tbs. worcestershire sauce*

Place tenderloin in a casserole dish that has a lid. Combine remaining ingredients, mix and pour over meat. Place lid on the dish and bake in 150C oven for 1 hour. Cut meat into 1 inch slices and use the soup as flavoursome gravy.

Pork Tenderloin with Mustard Sauce

Serves 6. This is a great Dinner Party Main …

- *600g pork tenderloin*
- *¼ cup soy sauce*
- *¼ cup bourbon*
- *2 tbs. brown sugar*

Mix soy sauce, bourbon and sugar. Marinate pork in the mixture for 2-3 hours, basting occasionally. Remove pork and bake in a preheated 150C oven for 1 hour, basting occasionally. Remove and slice.

Optional: This is sensational served with the mustard sauce.

Rich Tomato Pork

Serves 4. A recipe from Tanya Ormsby.

- *4 pork chops*
- *2 cloves garlic, crushed*
- *420g tin of seasoned diced tomatoes, e.g. basil and garlic, or oregano and basil*
- *½ cup cream*

In a non-stick pan fry pork until golden on both sides, add garlic and tinned tomatoes, bring to boil then let simmer for 2.5 hours (you may need a little more tomato mixture, depending on size of fillets).   Half an hour before serving, add cream and turn up the heat to thicken.

Optional: Serve with mashed potatoes and beans with pine nuts.

Roast Pork

Serves 8. From Lisa Darr. This continues to stand the test of time, a classic always does!

- *1 kg roast leg of pork*
- *3 tbs extra virgin olive oil*

Preheat oven 220C. Rub 1 tbs. oil onto rind of pork. Grind sea salt over rind and rub into pork. Pour remaining oil into baking dish and place in 220C oven for 20 minutes. Reduce heat to 180C and cook for 1 hour (or half hour per 500g).

*Optional: Serve with roast vegetables, best gravy ever and apple sauce. Kim's husband, Glen scores the skin, lathers it with fresh lemon juice and loads of ground sea salt ... **Makes a divine crackling!***

Sausage Bake

Serves 4. So easy, so tasty, so cheap!

- *6 thick sausages*
- *2 cups of chopped vegetables (celery, onion, carrot, broccoli, cauliflower, etc.)*
- *½ cup tasty cheese, grated*
- *420g can cream of mushroom soup*

Combine all in a casserole dish and season with sea salt and pepper. Bake covered for 45 minutes at 150C, uncover, stir and bake a further 15 minutes.

Sunshine State Baked Pork

Serves 4

- *4 pork chops*
- *2 tbs. brown sugar*
- *2 cups crushed pineapple*
- *3 medium sweet potatoes (orange ones)*

Place the pineapple with its juice into a casserole dish. Place the sliced sweet potato over the pineapple and sprinkle with brown sugar. Place the pork chops on top of the sweet potatoes. Cover with lid or alfoil and bake for 1 hour at 150C, and then uncovered for 10 minutes at 200C.

Tangy Pork Chops

Serves 4

- *4 pork chops*
- *½ cup honey*
- *¼ cup Worcestershire sauce*
- *¼ cup tomato sauce*

Lightly brown pork chops under grill. Place in a shallow baking dish. Combine remaining ingredients and pour over chops. Cover and bake at 170C for 45 minutes.

Vegetarian Mains

Girls are like phones: We love to be held, talked to; but if you press the wrong button you'll be disconnected!

Anonymous

Baked Ravioli

Serves 4-6

- *1 pkt fresh ravioli*
- *500g of organic pasta sauce (leave aside 200g)*
- *3 cups parmesan cheese, grated (leave aside 1 cup for topping)*
- *2 sprigs parsley, chopped*

Preheat oven to 190C. Cook ravioli in boiling water until it is just cooked, drain. Line a casserole dish with a thin layer of pasta sauce, add a layer of ravioli and sprinkle a layer of cheese and a touch of parsley. Repeat layering process finishing with a layer of ravioli, topped with remaining pasta sauce, and a sprinkling of the last cup of cheese. Bake for 15 minutes or until cheese is melted and bubbly. Cut into squares as you would lasagne.

Optional: Serve hot with salad, homemade potato chips or just by itself.

Cheesy, Cabbage Pasta Bake

Serves 4

- *2 cups penne pasta, cooked*
- *Savoy cabbage, shredded*
- *1 cup tasty cheese, grated*
- *2 slices of buttered bread finely grated*

Preheat the oven to 220C. In a baking dish, place alternating layers of pasta, cabbage and cheese and season between layers. Sprinkle with breadcrumbs and cheese and bake in a 180C oven for 10-15 minutes or until bubbling.

Green Coconut Curry

Serves 4 and is really, really tasty!

- *4 tbs. green curry paste*
- *400ml can coconut milk*
- *1.5 cups mixed sweet potato*
- *1.5 cups mixed vegetables*
  (broccoli, carrots, zucchinis, green beans, etc.)

Heat a wok or a deep frying pan (with a lid) to low heat. Add the green curry paste and gently stir-fry for a minute or so. Add the sweet potato and coconut milk with 1 cup water. Cover with a lid, and bring to the boil and gently simmer until the sweet potato is almost cooked. Add your mixed vegetables (exclude soft vegies, like zucchini and squash, etc.) and continue to simmer for another 10 minutes. When the sweet potato is starting to fall apart, add soft vegetables. Simmer for another 5 minutes. When all vegetables are cooked and the sweet potato has broken down to almost a puree, the dish is ready.

Optional: This is delicious served over rice and is nice with chicken, as well.

Green Bean Curry

Serves 4. Tis easy and yummy.

- *500g fresh green beans*
- *2 tbs. red curry paste*
- *1 red capsicum or a can of bamboo shoots*
  or any other vegies you have in the fridge, if desired!
- *6 cups chicken stock*

Top and tail the beans and cut in half or thirds, if really long. In a saucepan heat the curry paste stirring continuously for approx. 1 minute. Add chicken stock and beans and bring to a rapid boil. Cook for 15 - 20 minutes; halfway through, add capsicum. Continue to cook until the beans are well done and have absorbed the flavour of the curry-chicken broth. Serve over rice.

Mushroom Risotto

Serves 4

- *300g mushrooms, chopped*
- *2 cups arborio rice*
- *1 ltr chicken or vegetable stock*
- *1 cup parmesan cheese, shaved*

Lightly fry mushrooms in a non-stick pan. Add rice, stir until combined. Put stock in another pan and boil. Stir 2/3 cup stock into the rice. Stir until all absorbed. Continue adding stock in small quantities, stirring regularly, until gone. When this process is finished, add cheese and season.

Optional: Add a chopped onion with mushrooms.

Original Risotto

Serves 4

- 2 tbs. olive oil
- 1.5 tbs. butter
- 200g arborio rice
- 5 cups of stock

Simmer the stock on the stove. In a separate, heavy-based saucepan, heat the oil and butter. Add the rice and stir to coat with the oil and butter. Stir for 2 minutes until you hear a cracking sound and the rice becomes translucent. Add ½ cup of the stock and stir until it is absorbed. Continue adding more liquid in this manner until the rice is cooked. Taste after 15-20 minutes. The rice should be firm to the bight. Remove from the heat, add whatever flavourings you want. Season and stir.

Optional fillings; pumpkin and feta, semi-dried tomato & baby spinach, pea & pecorino.

Pasta with Tomato & Basil

Serves 4. The kids will love this, too.

- 2 cups of pasta
- 400ml Italian sugo (tomato pasta sauce)
- ½ cup freshly chopped basil leaves
- ½ cup parmesan cheese, shaved

Cook the pasta on high for only 8 minutes, drain, and add to the simmering sugo and most of the parmesan. When the pasta is al dente, stir though the basil leaves and serve with remaining parmesan and a basil leaf on top.

Sour Cream Quiche

Serves 4-6

- *1 sheet puffed pastry*
- *3 eggs*
- *300ml sour cream*
- *Filling; choose from feta, tinned corn, asparagus, baby spinach, semi-dried tomatoes, bacon, onion, tuna, chicken*

Line a rubber pie dish (doesn't require greasing) with puffed pastry. Beat eggs and sour cream. Pour over chosen filling. To taste, add sea salt and pepper and bake in a 180C oven for 30 minutes or until set.

Optional: Kim's Mummy often adds a drop of tomato and worcestershire sauces to the egg mix for extra flavour.

Desserts

"Kindness is like sugar, it makes life taste a little sweeter!"

Carla Yerovi

Apple Crumble

Serves 4-6. A golden oldie … This is really easy and really tasty!

- *1 can apple pie filling*
- *¼ - ½ cup soft butter*
- *¾ cup brown sugar*
- *1 cup plain flour*

Place apple filling into a baking dish. Sprinkle with 2 tbs. of brown sugar. Mix remaining ingredients in a bowl (reserving 2 tbs. butter) with a knife until crumbly. Sprinkle on top of apple filling and drizzle with reserved melted butter. Bake in a 200C oven for 30 minutes, or until the crumble is a golden brown.

Optional: Add ½ tsp. mixed spice to the apple mix. Serve with custard or ice-cream.

Apricot Turnovers

Makes 4. A recipe from Katherine Knight.

- *1 sheet puffed pastry, thawed*
- *4 ripe apricots*
- *4 tbs apricot jam*
- *2 tbs icing sugar*

Preheat oven 180C. Place puffed pastry onto a baking sheet and quarter. Cut apricots and evenly place them and the jam in the middle of the 4 quarters. Fold to form a triangle pressing to seal all edges with a fork. Make small diagonal cuts across the top of the dough.   Bake for 20 minutes or until golden brown. Cool then dust with icing sugar.

Barbie Bananas

Serves 4. A recipe from Tanya Ormsby.

- *4 bananas*
- *½ cup baileys Irish cream (or imitation)*
- *4 scoops ice-cream*

Put the whole bananas on the BBQ - skins and all! Leave for 4-5 minutes, slit the top and add enough Baileys to prevent overflowing. Leave for a further 1-2 minutes, remove and serve with ice-cream.

Basic Cheesecake

Serves 8

- *250g cream cheese, softened*
- *1 sachet gelatine*
- *395g can condensed milk*
- *Bickie base (as follows)*

In medium bowl, beat cream cheese until smooth. Add condensed milk and mix until combined. Dissolve gelatine in 3 tbs. of boiling water, stirring vigorously until dissolved; then add to mixture. Pour into above bickie base and chill for at least 1 hour prior to serving.

Optional: Delicious covered with fresh strawberries and kiwi fruit.

Bickie Base

- *¾ pkt sweet bickies*
- *5 tbs. butter melted*

Blend the bickies in a blender or food processor. Transfer to a bowl and add the melted butter. Mix well and then press into the bottom of a cheesecake dish. Chill before using.

Optional: Add a dash of nutmeg for flavour.

Blackcurrant Ice Cream

Serves 4

- *1 tin organic blackcurrants in juice*
  (or even better, 2 punnets of fresh or frozen blackcurrants)
- *½ cup fructose*
- *600ml organic plain yoghurt*

Place blackcurrants and juice with the fructose in a medium saucepan and heat until the sugar has dissolved. Remove from heat and combine the yoghurt and blackcurrant mixture in a separate mixing bowl and allow to cool. Once cooled, transfer to a freezer-safe container with lid and freeze until set (approx. 2 hours). During this process you will need to take the ice cream out of the freezer and stir every ½ hour to ensure it sets well.

Blue Chockie Mousse

Serves 4. This is berry, berry nice!

- *1 punnet blueberries*
- *200g dark chocolate*
- *300ml thickened cream*

Evenly place blueberries into the bottom of four small ramekins. Melt chocolate carefully in a bowl in the microwave, stir every 15 seconds. Remove and allow to cool. Beat cream until soft peaks form, then fold in the melted chocolate. Spoon the mixture over the blueberries and serve immediately.

Blueberry Puffs

Makes 4

- 2 sheets puff pastry, thawed
- 1 punnet blueberries
- 1 cup caster sugar
- ¼ cup melted butter

Preheat oven to 180C. Cut pastry in ½, allowing for 4 pieces. Thoroughly combine blueberries and ¾ of the sugar, and then place in the center of the pastry, roll up and brush with butter. Make a few fine cuts on the top and sprinkle with remaining sugar. Place on a lined baking tray and bake for 15-20 minutes, or until golden brown.

Optional: Serve warm with a scoop of creamy, vanilla ice-cream.

Brisk Apricot Brulee

Serves 6

- ½ cup apricot jam
- 425g can apricot halves in juice
- 600 ml carton ready made custard
- ½ - ¾ cup brown sugar

Drain all but about 3 tbs. of juice from apricots. Chop apricots roughly. Mix apricots and jam together and spoon into the bottom of six half-cup ramekins. Stand ramekins in a baking tray with its bottom covered by water. Divide custard evenly among ramekins. Sprinkle with thick layer of sugar over the top of the custard and grill until sugar melts and turns golden.

Optional: Could substitute apricots for strawberries or mixed berries and their jams.

Chocolate Mousse

Serves 4. This is a dreamy Chocolate Mousse.

- ½ cup quality dark chocolate
- 1 tbs. butter
- 2 eggs
- ½ cup thickened cream

Melt chocolate with butter carefully in a bowl in the microwave, stir every 15 seconds until smooth. Remove and cool for a few minutes, then stir in 2 beaten egg yolks and half a cup lightly whipped cream. Whip 2 eggwhites until soft peaks form, then gently fold into chocolate mixture. Spoon into small dishes or glasses and refrigerate for 3 hours, or until firm.

Optional: Drizzle 1 tsp. of Grand Marnier, cognac or rum over each mousse. Serve with extra whipped cream and fresh raspberries and strawberries, dusted with icing sugar.

Chrissie's Caramel Tart

Serves 6. Recipe by Joy – Rachael's Mum.

- 1 sheet sweet short crust pastry
- 400g can Nestle Top n Fill caramel
- 1 cup thickened cream, whipped
- 1 tsp. butter

Preheat oven to 180C. Grease pie dish with butter and line with sheet of pastry. Place in oven for 10 minutes, or until golden brown. Pour caramel into pastry shell. Spoon over thickened whipped cream generously ... As easy as 1,2,3!

Coconut- Ripe Ice Cream

Morgan, Kim's 4 year old calls this, "Cocolicious!"

- *2 cups desiccated coconut*
- *2 litres vanilla ice-cream*
- *2 cherry ripes*
- *165g can coconut cream*

Toast coconut in a frying pan over a medium heat, tossing regularly, until just beginning to colour. Remove from heat. Cut cherry ripes into small, uneven pieces. Soften ice-cream. Mix toasted coconut, cherry ripes and coconut cream into ice cream. Refreeze in a loaf tin, or back in the original plastic ice-cream container.

Creme Brulee

Serves 4

- *400ml cream*
- *1 vanilla bean, split and scraped*
- *5 egg yolks*
- *½ - ¾ cup brown sugar*

Combine cream and vanilla bean in a medium saucepan and bring just to boil. Leave to infuse for 15 minutes. Meanwhile, lightly beat egg yolks and half the sugar until well combined. Strain infused cream over yolk mixture and whisk briefly to blend. Return cream and egg mixture to same cleaned saucepan and stir over very low heat until custard thickens enough to coat the back of a spoon. Pour into 4 ramekins and refrigerate, covered for about 4 hours. Just before serving, remove from fridge and place in a baking tray full of cold water and ice. Cover surface of each brulee generously with remaining sugar. Place under grill until sugar melts, making a shiny crust, or use a blow torch to brown if you have one.

The top should be hard, and when cracked with the spoon, will give a wonderful contrast to the creamy bottom.

Fondue

Serves 2

- *1 cup milk chocolate*
- *½ cup lite cream*

Break chocolate and put into fondue pot with cream. Stir well and heat gently, stirring until chocolate is melted.

Optional: Serve with a plate of fresh fruit, marshmallows, etc.

Frozen Fruit Yoghurt Soft Serve

Serves 4-6. A recipe from Cyndi O'Meara.

- *2 cups fresh fruit (bananas, strawberries, mango, blueberries, etc.), all roughly chopped*
- *½ cup manuka honey*
- *2.5 cups of organic natural yoghurt*

Process fruit in a blender until smooth. Add honey and yoghurt and mix thoroughly. Pour into a covered container and freeze. Remove from freezer 20-30 minutes before serving.

Fruit Sundae Snacks

Makes 6

- *12 strawberries, washed, hulled and chopped*
- *3 cups of fruit, chopped (such as cherries, apples, bananas, seedless grapes, kiwifruit, peaches)*
- *6 waffle cones*
- *1 tbs. shredded coconut*

Blend the strawberries till smooth, and set aside. Place the fruit in a bowl and toss to combine. Spoon fruit evenly among the cones. Drizzle with strawberry puree, top with coconut and serve.

Grilled Mango Halves with Lime

Serves 4

- *3 large mangoes*
- *1 lime*
- *2 tbs. brown sugar*

Cut each mango in half, cutting around the seed and leaving the skin on. Score the skin of each half with a sharp knife making an X pattern. Squeeze lime juice onto the mango halves. Sprinkle the fruit with the brown sugar. Place the mangoes on a preheated and oiled BBQ plate and cook, sugared side down, for 2-3 minutes.

Optional: Serve with a sorbet. A great BBQ dessert.

Ice Cream with a Twist

Serves 2

- *2 bowls of vanilla ice-cream*
- *1 punnet strawberries, washed and hulled*
- *2 tbs. caramelised balsamic vinegar*

Place vanilla ice-cream in a bowl. Slice strawberries and mix with caramelised balsamic vinegar. Once combined, tip over ice-cream and serve.

Key Lime Pie

Serves 8. This is DELECTABLE!!

- *4 large egg yolks*
- *400g can of condensed milk*
- *4 limes, juiced*
- *Bickie base*

Use an electric mixer and beat the egg yolks until they are thick and turn to a light yellow – don't over mix. Turn the mixer off and add the condensed milk. Turn speed to low and mix in half of the lime juice. Once the juice is incorporated, add the other half and the zest of one lime, continue to mix until blended (just a few seconds). Pour the mixture into the bickie base and bake for 12 minutes at 150C to set.

Optional: Serve with whipped cream.

Microwave Fondue

Serves 2. Always looking for quick and tasty desserts, we devised this fantastic little treat.

- *1 cup dark chocolate*
- *½ cup lite cream*
- *2 tbs. orange zest*

Warm cream and orange zest in a saucepan, slowly.
Break chocolate and melt in microwave, checking every 15 seconds.
When melted add to warm cream. Stir well and when warm pour into a bowl.

Optional: Serve with a plate of strawberries, bananas, kiwi fruit and orange – all sliced.

Pavlova

Serves 6-8

- *2 tsp. cornflour*
- *1 cup of caster sugar*
- *1 tsp. vanilla*
- *4 eggwhites*

Preheat the oven to 180C. Line a baking tray with baking paper.
Beat the eggwhites until soft peaks form and gradually beat in the sugar. Beat until the mixture is thick and the sugar is dissolved.
Carefully fold in the cornflour and vanilla essence. Spoon onto the baking paper on the tray. Reduce the oven heat to 150C and place in oven, bake for 1 hour.

For best result: Eggs should be at room temperature.

Optional: Allow to cool completely before decorating with the whipped cream and sliced fruit. Karen Fitzgerald told us that this works just as well … "If you don't have cornflour, use vinegar"!

Pecan Ice Cream with Maple Syrup

Makes 4. A recipe from Shane McCosker.

- *2 tbs. icing sugar*
- *1 cup pecan nuts, roughly chopped*
- *1.5 cups creamy vanilla ice-cream*
- *2 tbs. maple syrup*

Heat the oven to 180C. Mix the icing sugar with the pecans on a baking tray and sprinkle with a little water to make a thickish paste. Bake in the oven for a few minutes, or until toasted and caramelised. Scoop out the ice cream into 4 glasses or bowls, sprinkle with pecans, then drizzle with maple syrup.

Poached Pears

Serves 6. A recipe from Wendy Beattie. Simply; a sweet success!

- *6 firm ripe, pears*
- *½ cup white wine*
- *Easy mocha sauces*

Peel skin from pears and place upright in a microwaveable bowl. Pour wine and 1/3 cup water over the pears, return lid and cook on high for 10 minutes, or until soft. Remove and allow to cool In wine Once cold, remove pears from wine and place in serving bowl, lavish with mocha sauce and serve.

Praline Fondue

Serves 4-6

- *½ cup caster sugar*
- *¾ cup toasted almonds*
- *2 cups cream*
- *2 tbs. cornflour*

Put caster sugar into a small saucepan, place over a low heat and leave until sugar is golden brown. Add almonds. Pour onto a lightly greased cake tin and allow to cool completely. Grind finely. Place cream into fondue pot, blend in cornflour and stir until thickened. Stir in praline. Serve with fresh fruit, marshmallows, etc.

Optional: Add a dash of vanilla essence to caster sugar to taste.

Profiteroles

Makes 14. This will delight, they are Delicious!!

- *1 pkt White Wings Decadent Chocolate Profiteroles*
- *3 eggs*
- *300 ml cream*
- *1 cup milk*

"Five Simple Steps" as per the packet.

Roasted Honey Pears with Honey Cream

Serves 4 and your mummy-in-law will love it, and you!!!!

- *3 firm, ripe pears*
- *½ cup honey*
- *2 tbs. brown sugar*
- *1.5 cups thickened cream, whipped*

Cut pears into quarters and remove cores. Place in an ovenproof dish, drizzle with ¼ cup honey and sprinkle with brown sugar. Pour ½ cup water around pears. Bake uncovered at 180C for 30 minutes, or until just soft. Place 3 pear quarters on four serving plates. Drizzle pan juices over pears. Mix whipped cream and ¼ cup honey together until combined. Serve over pears.

Optional: Add ¼ tsp. cinnamon to cream and honey for a lovely flavour.

For The Children

Children are one third of our population and all of our future.

Select Panel for the Promotion of Child Health, 1981

Savoury

Bugs in Rugs

Makes 12

- *3 slices brown bread*
- *½ cup tomato sauce*
- *¼ cup butter, melted*
- *12 cocktail frankfurters*

Preheat oven 180C. Pierce frankfurters all over with a fork. Spread tomato sauce on bread, then cut into quarters. Place a frankfurter diagonally on each quarter of bread. Bring up edges and secure with a toothpick. Brush liberally with the melted butter. Place on greased baking tray and bake for 10 minutes until bread Is crisp and lightly brown. Serve warm.

Optional: Sprinkle with poppy seeds before baking.

Cheesy Bears

Makes 12

- *12 slices bread*
- *2 tbs. butter*
- *12 slices of cheese*
- *1 tbs. vegemite*

Lightly butter bread; place cheese on buttered side. Using a teddie bear cookie cutter, cut a bear shape from each slice. Using a chopstick end, dip into vegemite and draw teddy bear faces onto cheese. Chill prior to serving.

Cheese Bickies

Makes 12

- *1 cup tasty cheese, grated*
- *1 cup rice flour*
- *3 tbs. ground almonds*
- *1 tbs. margarine*

Rub margarine into the rice and ground almonds, and add the cheese. Add a little water, if required, to make into a stiff dough. Roll out on a floured surface and cut into shapes. Bake at 100C for 10 to 15 minutes, or until golden.

Egg in a Hole

Makes 1

- ¼ tbs. butter
- 1 slice brown bread
- 1 free-range egg

Heat frying pan and melt butter, cut a hole in the bread to fit the egg. Place bread in frying pan and crack egg into hole. Cook on one side until it just firms, flip and cook until done.

Fish Cocktails

Makes 24. Morgan 4, Jaxson 1 and Hamilton 1 love these!

- 250g fresh white fish fillets
- 3 tbs. plain flour
- 1 eggwhite
- 1.25 cup cornflake crumbs

Preheat oven 180C. Cut fish into 3 cm cubes. Coat in flour and shake off excess. Whisk eggwhite in small bowl. Dip fish, one piece at a time in eggwhite, coat with cornflake crumbs. Place in a single layer on an oven tray and bake for 15 minutes, or until golden.

Gourmet Baked Beans on Toast

- *4 thick slices bread, crust removed*
- *400g can baked beans*
- *2 tsp. butter*
- *½ cup cheddar cheese, grated*

Preheat oven 220C. Butter both sides of bread slices and press into 4 holes of a muffin tray. Bake for 5-10 minutes or until the bread is crisp and golden. Heat the baked beans in a pan over low heat until just warm. Spoon the baked beans into the bread cup and sprinkle with the grated cheese.

Italian Chicken

Makes 4-6.

- *2 chicken breasts*
- *2 tbs. extra virgin olive oil*
- *1 onion, chopped*
- *1 jar spaghetti sauce with roasted vegetables*

Tenderise breasts, slice, then brown in oil. Push to one side and sauté onion until tender. Stir in spaghetti sauce and cover pan. Simmer for 10-12 minutes or until chicken is tender, and serve with pasta.

Mini Hotdogs

Makes 8

- *1 sheet puff pastry*
- *1 egg, beaten*
- *8 cocktail frankfurters*
- *Tomato sauce to serve*

Cut thawed pastry into 8 pieces. Brush with beaten egg before placing a frankfurter across each pastry piece. Wrap opposite ends of pastry around the frankfurter. Brush with egg again. Bake in 180C for 10-15 minutes or until golden. Serve with a bowl of tomato sauce for dipping.

MiniPizzas

Makes 2. Thanks, Michelle Fredericks.

- *2 English muffins sliced in half*
- *4 tsp. pizza paste*
- *3 rashers of bacon*
- *4 tbs. mozzarella cheese*

Slice English muffin in half, spread pizza paste; lightly fry bacon pieces and scatter on top of paste and top with cheese grill until golden brown... quick and easy!

Parmesan Twists

- *1 sheet puff pastry*
- *4 tbs. parmesan cheese, grated*

Smother the sheet of puff pastry with parmesan. Cut in half, and then cut into 2 cm wide strips. Twist and bake in a hot oven for approximately 5 minutes or until golden brown. Allow to cool and store in an airtight container. For an added flavour, you can sprinkle with paprika prior to baking.

Vegemite Twists

- *1 sheet puff pastry*
- *1 tbs. vegemite*

Exactly as above, except substitute parmesan with vegemite (no paprika).

Vegetable Shapes

Serves 2. These put a thrill into eating vegetables!

- *1 potato*
- *100g piece pumpkin*
- *Extra virgin macadamia oil spray*
- *Metal shapes eg., stars, hearts, animal shapes etc*

Slice potato and pumpkin into 2cm thick slices. Cut out as many shapes as possible. Spray with oil and bake in 180C oven 15-20 minutes, turning halfway through.

Optional: Keep scraps and make a mashed potato and pumpkin on another night.

Pizza

Serves 4

Base
- *1 cup of Simply No Knead Gluten Free Bread mix*
  (available in health food section of all leading supermarkets)
- *¾ cup of water*

Topping
- *140g tub of pizza sauce*
- *Mozzarella cheese*

Preheat oven 180C. Mix bread mix and water with beater, on medium speed, until well combined. Spread over alfoil on a pizza tray, patting mixture into the shape of the tray with your fingers. Spread pizza sauce evenly and top with whatever yummies your little darlings will eat. Sprinkle with cheese and bake in 180C oven for 15 -20 minutes.

Popcorn Chicken

Serves 4

- *4 chicken breasts*
- *1-2 tbs. cajun powder*
- *1.5 cups of basmati rice*
- *½ cup of extra virgin olive oil*

Bring a medium saucepan with 3 cups of water to boil. Add rice and simmer till cooked, drain and set aside. Tenderise chicken lightly and cut into small pieces. Put into a frying pan with oil and stir over a medium heat. Before chicken has whitened, shake on cajun powder to taste. Leave cooking until well done and crispy black (looks burnt but tastes yummy). Serve with rice.

Porcupines

Serves 4. From our Grade 8 Home Ec. class – *they're great!!*

- *½ kg mince*
- *½ cup half cooked rice*
- *1 egg*
- *440g can condensed tomato soup*

Combine mince, egg and rice in a bowl and mix well. Season with sea salt and pepper. Roll mixture into small rissole like balls = 'Porcupines'. Place in casserole dish. Mix tomato soup with ¾ of same can of water and pour over porcupines. Cook in moderate oven for about 1 hour. Serve with mashed potato and vegetables.

Optional: Add an onion, finely chopped, to the mince for a yummy flavour

Sandwich Rollups

- *4 slices brown bread*
- *1 tbs. butter*
- *Sandwich fillings; ham, cheese, vegemite, cheese, etc*
- *Bunch of fresh, long chives*

Remove crusts. Lay slices of bread on a flat surface and, with a rolling pin; roll out until bread is quite thin. Butter lightly and cover each slice with chosen fillings. Roll tightly and cut into thirds. Tie with a chive.

Savoury Dip

- *2.5 cups sour cream*
- *1 pkt chicken soup mix*
- *Food colourings*
- *Assortment of julienne vegies*

Combine sour cream and soup mix. Separate mixture into three small bowls and tint with whatever food colourings you have. Serve with julienne vegies.

Simple Spaghetti

Serves 2. A recipe by Heather and Alexis Wallis …Your kids will love it, too!

- *½ packet of penne pasta*
- *1 tbs. butter*
- *½ cup cheddar cheese*
- *½ cup tomato sauce*

Cook pasta, drain and place in saucepan. Add butter mixing until melted. Add tomato sauce and cheese and mix until cheese starts to melt. Serve hot.

Optional: Sprinkle with toasted pine nuts.

Spaghetti Bolognese

Serves 6

- *1 packet of thin spaghetti pasta*
- *2 cups lean mince*
- *500g of mushroom or vegetable pasta sauce*
  (We use the black and gold pasta sauce a Chef introduced
  it to us as one of the yummier on the market ... & cheaper!!)
- *1 cup parmesan cheese, shaved*

Put 2 tbs. of water in a frying pan and add mince; cook on medium heat till pink colouring has just disappeared. Add pasta sauce and stir, lowering heat and covering for 6 minutes. Boil water and add spaghetti to boil, simmer for 8 minutes, or until al dente. Drain pasta and place equal portions of pasta in 4 bowls. Add mince on top. Sprinkle with cheese to finish.

Sweet Chicken with Cornflakes

Serves 4-6. Recipe from Cyndi O'Meara. This is a real hit!

- *750g organic chicken breast fillets*
- *¾ cup organic plain yoghurt*
- *2 cups cornflakes, ground*
- *1 cup parmesan cheese, finely grated*

Preheat oven to 180C. Combine cornflakes and cheese together in one bowl, and place yoghurt in another bowl. Coat chicken with yoghurt and then cornflake and cheese mixture. Bake in oven for 20-30 minutes, depending on size of chicken breasts.

Too Easy Chicken Nuggets

Serves 2. These are requested at least twice a week!

- 2 chicken breasts, cut into bight size pieces
- 1.5 cups organic breadcrumbs
- 1.5 cups organic mayonnaise
- 1 tbs. butter melted

Preheat oven to 180C. Coat chicken with mayonnaise and roll in breadcrumbs. Lay on a baking paper lined baking tray. Drizzle with a little butter and bake for 20 minutes.

Tuna With Spaghetti

Makes 2. A recipe from the lovely Alice Beattie!

- 420g tin spaghetti
- 400g tin tuna chunks, drained
- ½ cup grated cheese
- ½ cup breadcrumbs

Combine tuna and spaghetti. Place in baking dish. Sprinkle with cheese and breadcrumbs and bake in moderate oven until golden brown.

Vegetable Lasagne

Serves 6. Thanks to Kimmy Morrison for this terrific and very easy dinner!

- *6 sheets lasagna pasta*
- *3 cups shredded cheese*
- *1 sweet potato*
- *500g jar of vegetable pasta sauce*

Preheat oven to 150C. Peel and slice sweet potato then boil till soft, drain liquid and mash. Line a baking tray with baking paper. Place 2 sheets of lasagna side by side. Lightly cover with layer of cheese. Spoon over some mashed potato - covering cheese. Pour over pasta sauce to cover mash potato. Repeat layering process till last lasagna sheet has been used and cheese, potato and sauce has been laid over the top of the last sheet. Finish off with ½ cup of cheese. Bake for 35 minutes, or until cheese is slightly golden.

Optional: Fabulous with salad, chips or even more vegetables.

Sweets

The laughter of a child is the light of a house.
(Anonymous)

Apple Turnovers

Serves 8. Another quick and easy recipe from Meredith Mullally.

* *2 sheets of puff pastry*
* *1 tin pie apple with cinnamon*
* *2 tbs. milk*

Cut the puff pasty into quarters. Fill one side of the quarter with pie apple, then fold into turnovers. Glaze with milk for a golden finish and bake in a hot oven for 10 minutes.

Apricot Dream Balls

Makes 24. Paul Bermingham's favourites!!!

* *¾ cup dried fruit medley*
* *¼ cup dried apricots*
* *1 tbs. coconut milk*
* *Plate of desiccated coconut*

Place fruit medley, apricots and coconut milk into a food processor or your handheld mixer, and whiz until mixture comes together. Shape into balls and roll in coconut. Chill until firm.

Optional: We have used condensed milk and tahini instead of coconut milk and both were yummy.

Baked Custard

Serves 4. A recipe from our muchly loved 'Grandma', Jennette McCosker.

- *2 cups milk*
- *2 eggs*
- *2 tbs. raw sugar*
- *½ tsp. vanilla essence*

Put milk and sugar in a saucepan; bring to the boil, stirring occasionally. Add vanilla essence and remove from heat. Pour about ¼ cup of boiling milk into beaten eggs - while stirring. This warms the eggs and prevents curdling. Pour the egg mixture into the remaining milk mixture. Stir briskly until well combined. Pour into a small baking dish and bake in a basin of water in a 150C oven for about 1 hour.

Optional: Sprinkle with nutmeg prior to baking.

Bananas in Mars

Serves 4. A recipe from the inventive Anthony 'Spud' Moore " Great when camping" were his words.

- *4 firm bananas*
- *2 mars bars*

Cut a slice in the banana skin half way down its middle. Slice up mars bars and poke into the slit. Wrap in alfoil and place in oven or on the BBQ and cook for approximately 3-5 minutes. Remove and turn out onto a plate.

Optional: This is really delicious served with a little pouring cream.

Blancmange

Serves 4. A recipe from Jocelyn Wilson.

- *1 tin evaporated milk*
- *1 cup of fruit*
- *2 tbs. honey*
- *1 sachet of gelatine*

Mix milk, fruit and honey together. Dissolve the gelatine in 3 tbs. of boiling water and add to the mixture, stirring well. Pour into individual bowls. Allow to set in the fridge for a couple of hours.

Optional: Substitute 1 cup of fruit with 1 cup of chocolate topping for a change.

Caramel Bumps

Makes 10

- *200g caramel buds*
- *10 milk arrowroot bickies*
- *20 small, white marshmallows*
- *¾ cup desiccated coconut*

Melt caramel in microwave. Spread a small amount on each biscuit. Before it sets, place two marshmallows on each biscuit. Allow to set. Dip bickie into remaining caramel to coat marshmallows and tops of bickies. Sprinkle with coconut. Allow to set.

Chocolate Balls

A recipe loved by Matthew, Brady & Harry McCosker

- *1 pkt sweet biscuits, crushed*
- *3 tbs. cocoa*
- *¾ cup condensed milk*
- *½ cup desiccated coconut*

Mix crushed biscuit, cocoa and condensed milk together to make a sticky consistency. Using a generous tsp. of mixture, roll into balls and cover in coconut. Chill before serving. These can also be frozen.

Chocolate Bananas

Makes 6

- *¾ cup milk chocolate*
- *3 bananas*

Melt chocolate in microwave, check every 15 seconds and stir. Remove skin and slice bananas in half. Roll in melted chocolate and place on a tray for cooling. Chill before serving.

Chocolate Dipped Fruit

Serves 4

- 2.5 cups milk chocolate melts
- 2 bananas, thickly sliced
- 1 cup strawberries, washed and hulled
- ¾ cup dried apricots

Line baking tray with baking paper. Place melts in microwave-safe bowl and cook on high, stirring every 15 seconds, until melted. Using your hand, dip fruit, one piece at a time, into chocolate to coat about ¾ of each piece of fruit. Place fruit in single layer on baking tray, refrigerate until set.

Chocolate Nut Clusters

Makes 24

- ¼ cup shelled, unsalted pistachios
- ¼ cup slivered almonds
- 1 cup milk chocolate melts
- ½ cup sultanas

Line baking tray with baking paper. Heat small heavy-base frying pan, toast pistachios and almonds, stirring constantly, until browned lightly (take care not to scorch nuts because they burn easily). Remove nuts from hot pan. Place melts in microwave-safe bowl and cook on high, stirring every 15 seconds, until melted. Stir nuts and sultanas into chocolate. Use a heaped tablespoon to scoop out the chocolate mixture, drop onto prepared tray. Refrigerate, uncovered, until set.

Crunchy Banana on a Stick

Serves 2 and are nutritious and delicious!!

- 1 banana, cut lengthways in half
- 2 skewers
- ½ cup of organic full milk banana or vanilla yoghurt
- ½ cup of crushed crunchie cookie – any will do, as long as they're crunchy

Thread each banana half onto a skewer. Spread with some yoghurt and roll in cookie crumbs.

Cyndi's Real Custard

Serves 4-6. Recipe from Cyndi O'Meara

- 3 organic free-range eggs, beaten
- 2 cups organic milk
- ¼ cup organic sugar (or rapadura sugar)
- 1 tsp. vanilla essence

Combine eggs, milk and sugar in a saucepan, stir over medium heat (not too hot or custard will separate) until it coats the back of a metal spoon. Transfer immediately into a glass bowl standing in cold water. Add vanilla, stirring occasionally, while it cools.

Edible Pink Bracelets

Makes 6. Little girls absolutely adore these!

- *2 punnets of strawberries*
- *½ watermelon, seeded*
- *½ pkt pink marshmallows*
- *½ pkt raspberries*

Cut watermelon into large cubes. Thread strawberries, watermelon cubes and sweets onto string. Tie the ends in a bow.

Egg Custard

Makes 2 cups. This is delicious with prune snow!

- *2 cups milk*
- *5 tbs. caster sugar*
- *2 egg yolks*
- *2 tbs. cornflour*

Bring the milk and 2 tbs. sugar to boil in a saucepan over a medium heat. Whisk the yolks and remaining sugar together; then gradually fold in the cornflour to form a pale yellow paste. Carefully pour ½ of the boiled milk into the yolk mixture, whisking to incorporate. Return the remaining milk to the heat and bring to the boil, quickly whisk in the yolk mixture. Continue mixing until it returns to the boil. Transfer to a clean, dry bowl and cover the surface with cling wrap. Chill until required.

To use the custard once it has been chilled, beat until smooth. An electric beater gives a much smoother result than beating by hand.

Fluffy Pudding

Serves 4. A recipe from the lovely Gwen Colyer, our children adore this and it is so easy!!

- *1 pkt jelly*
- *375ml can evaporated milk*

Dissolve jelly in 1 cup boiling water, cool and add cold evaporated milk, beat until frothy. Place in the fridge until set.

Optional: Serve with whatever fruit compliments the flavour of the jelly.

Frozen Fruit Treats

Serves 4-6

- *1 cup strawberries, washed and hulled*
- *1 cup crushed pineapple*
- *2 bananas*
- *1 cup orange or apple juice*

Combine all ingredients into a blender and process till smooth. Pour into an ice block mould with paddle sticks or small paper cups and freeze. Serve partially defrosted, with a spoon if in a cup, or fully frozen if in a stick mould.

Fried Banana with Ice-Cream

Serves 2

- *2 ripe lady finger bananas*
- *2 tbs. butter*
- *1 tbs. raw sugar*
- *2 scoops vanilla ice-cream*

Preheat heavy frying pan, melt butter. Add bananas and sprinkle with raw sugar. Cook for 1 minute, turn and cook for a further minute, or until they reach desired doneness; serve each with a scoop of ice-cream.

Fruit Kebabs

Serves 4-6. Recipe from Jen Whittington.

- *1 packet skewers*
- *Choice of 2 fruits (berries, melon, citrus; whatever you have in the fridge or in the fruit basket)*
- *Choice of 1 tub of fruit yoghurt or 1 tbs. of organic honey*

Dice fruit into bight-size pieces (skin and clean, where required). Thread the chosen fruits alternatively onto a skewer, leaving enough room at the base so the skewer can be held. Drizzle with yoghurt or honey.

Homemade LCM'S

Serves 6

- *2.5 cups of rice bubbles*
- *½ cup of 100's & 1000's*
- *1.5 cups of marshmallows*
- *½ cup butter, melted, plus a little extra for greasing*

Mix rice bubbles, 100's and 1000's and 1 cup marshmallows, chopped, in a bowl. Melt remaining marshmallows, add butter and mix, then pour over ingredients, combining well. Pour into a greased tray and pat down. Place in fridge to set ... Remove, cut and serve!

Jelly Snow

Serves 4-6

- *1 pkt jelly (any flavour)*
- *1 cup frozen berries, partially thawed*
- *2 cups vanilla ice-cream*

Make up a packet of jelly and leave until almost set. Blend with a hand-held mixer or blender – it goes frothy and pale. Leave to set completely. Serve with purple ice cream – made by mixing berries through ice-cream.

Livened Ice-Cream

A recipe from our beloved Jan Neale – Nin.

- *1 pkt jelly (any flavour)*
- *Vanilla ice-cream*

Nin says "To 'liven' up ice-cream, sprinkle jelly crystals over the top. There are lots of flavours and colours; and a little goes a long way!"

Mars Bar Slice

Serves 6

- *3 mars bars*
- *4 tbs. butter, plus a little extra for greasing*
- *4 cups rice bubbles*

In a microwave proof dish, melt mars bars and butter for a couple of minutes. Add rice bubbles and mix well. Press into lightly greased tray. Refrigerate and cut into slices when ready to serve.

Marshmallow Medley

Serves 4. Another little treasure from Aine Watkins.

- *12 marshmallows*
- *¼ cup of sour cream*
- *4 mandarins*
- *1.5 tbs. coconut*

Mix all together with a spoon, chill and serve.

Mini-Muffins

Makes 12. You will be surprised how quick and easy these are.

- *1 cup self raising flour sifted*
- *1 cup thickened cream not whipped*
- *3 tbs. raw sugar*

Combine all ingredients and mix well. Pour into greased mini-muffin tray. Bake 10 minutes at 180C or until golden brown.

Mini White Chocolate Cups with Fruche & Strawberries

- *Cooking-oil spay*
- *1 cup white chocolate melts*
- *½ cup vanilla fruche*
- *6 large strawberries, finely chopped*

For best result, use 2.5cm paper patty-cake cases that have been lightly sprayed with cooking oil. Place chocolate in small heatproof bowl, place bowl over saucepan of simmering water, stirring until chocolate melts.   Using small pasty brush, paint chocolate thickly inside each case. Place paper cases on tray, refrigerate for 5 minutes. Brush cases with a second coat of chocolate; refrigerate another 5 minutes. Peel and discard paper cases. Meanwhile, combine fruche and strawberries in small bowl, place 1 level teaspoon of mixture into each chocolate case.

Rice Pudding

Serves 4. A recipe from the beautiful Mary Moore.

- *1 litre milk*
- *½ cup rice*
- *2 tbs. brown sugar*
- *½ tsp. vanilla essence*

Preheat oven. Add all ingredients to a baking dish place in the middle of a 150C oven and bake for 2 hours.

Popcorn Parcels

Makes 6

- *3 cups coloured popcorn*
- *1 cup white chocolate buttons*
- *½ liquorice strap, cut into long, thin strips*

Melt chocolate in the microwave until soft, check every 15 seconds and stir, add popcorn. Stir gently until well combined. Divide into six equal portions, shaping into a ball. Place on a tray and insert liquorice. Chill until firm.

Prune Snow

Serves 4 and is remembered as a favourite from my childhood!

- *1 cup prunes*
- *2 tbs. caster sugar*
- *2 eggwhites*

Place prunes into a saucepan and cover with water. Cook for approximately 10 minutes, or until soft. Remove from heat and allow to cool. Meanwhile, beat eggwhites until fluffy, add sugar, bit by bit, and continue to beat, until stiff. Remove seeds from prunes, and mash. Fold eggwhites into prunes and serve with custard (you can use your egg yolks to make a delicious egg custard).

Puffed Pastry with Nutella & Stewed Apples

Makes 8 . . . Yummy!

- *2 sheets puffed pasty*
- *8 tbs. Nutella*
- *2 cups stewed apples*
- *2 tbs. icing sugar*

Cut your puffed pastry sheets in quarters. Generously smear nutella diagonally from one end to the other. Place stewed apple along nutella. Fold opposite ends over mixture. Bake in preheated 180C oven for 15-20 minutes. Sprinkle with icing sugar for decoration.

Sesame & Honey Bars

Makes 12. These are made in a couple of minutes and are really tasty.

- *1 cup sesame seeds*
- *1 cup oatmeal*
- *½ cup manuka honey (or organic honey)*
- *½ cup butter, plus extra for greasing*

Preheat oven to 180C. Grind sesame seeds and oatmeal together in a food processor. Melt honey and butter in a small saucepan. Pour mixture into the food processor, Blend and turn out into a well-buttered baking tray (can line with baking paper instead of greasing the tray). Bake for 20-25 minutes, or until golden brown. Cut the biscuits in the tin and then leave them to cool.

Summer Yoghurt Treat

Serves 1

- ½ cup toasted fruit muesli
- 2 tbs. organic yoghurt
- 1 tbs. of mixed fruit (or fruit of choice, i.e. strawberries, banana, melon, grapes, blueberries, raspberries)

Place muesli in a glass or bowl. Top with yoghurt and sprinkle with mixed fruit.

Sweet Carrot Snacks

Serves 2-4

- 4 chilled carrots
- 2 tbs. organic manuka honey
- 1 tsp. sesame seeds

Peel chilled carrots, cut length by half, then slice into four. Add honey and sesame seeds to small side bowl. Great for after school. You can also use organic tahini as a substitute for honey.
A nutritious and healthy snack.

Sweet Toasted Sandwich

Serves 4.   A great idea from Meredith Mullally.

- *8 pieces of fruit bread*
- *420g can stewed apples*
- *1 tsp. cinnamon sugar*
- *1 tbs. butter*

Butter bread and turn upside down. Thickly coat 4 slices with apple and sprinkle with cinnamon sugar. Place remaining slices of buttered fruit bread, butter side up, on mixture. Toast as you would a normal toasted sandwich.

Optional: Serve plain or with ice-cream.

Toffees

Makes 12

- *2 cups sugar*
- *1 cup water*
- *1 tbs. vinegar*
- *100's & 1,000's*

Combine sugar, water and vinegar in a saucepan. Stir over medium heat until sugar has completely dissolved. Bring to the boil; reduce heat slightly. Boil without stirring for 20 minutes (it is ready when a drop of the mixture in cold water hardens). Pour into little patty cases and decorate with hundreds and thousands. Leave to set at room temperature.

Yummy Kebabs

Makes 6

- *1 punnet of strawberries, washed and hulled*
- *2 kiwi fruit*
- *3 bananas*
- *Assorted lollies*

Cut kiwi fruit and banana into chunks. Thread them, plus strawberries and lollies onto bamboo skewers.
Remove sharp ends before serving to children.

For The Lunch Box

Anyone who thinks the art of conversation is dead ought to tell a child to go to bed!!!

Robert Gallagher

A healthy school lunchbox is something we Mummy's try to aim for everyday. The best lunch is one that's nutritious and quick to prepare, but also fun and easy to eat. Encouraging your children to be involved in choosing foods and preparing their lunch can help ensure that it not only gets eaten, but enjoyed as well.

Fresh Fruit

With the price rises of late bananas, for example, are nearing the price of gold bullion ... in fact they may be just that!!!! However, if you shop wisely, you can still afford these and many more fresh fruit and vegetable ideas for the lunch boxes.

Our suggestion ... MARKETS!!! Locate your nearest markets and shop there. Generally, Not only are the prices of fresh fruit and vegetables MUCH CHEAPER they are usually home grown, organic, vine-ripened, TASTE SENSATIONAL and have a longer life.

- *Oranges – quartered*
- *Mandarins*
- *Apples: ask the vendor; which are the crunchy varieties at time of purchase as NO-ONE, least of all a child, likes a flowery apple! The skin of an apple is the best, nutrients-wise.*
- *Strawberries*
- *Bananas*
- *Grapes – white or black*
  (the skin of the black is FULL of great anti-oxidants!!)
- *Nectarine*

- *Peach / Plum*
- *Apricot*
- *Kiwi fruit*
- *Nashi – crunchy and juicy, our children love these*
- *Pear*
- *Orange, cut into quarters*
- *Passionfruit, cut in half*
- *Cubes of watermelon, honey dew or rockmelon*
- *Chunks of pineapple*
- *Mango(get stacks in season and freeze for outa season)*

Vegetable Sticks

- *Carrot sticks*
- *Celery sticks*
- *Cherry tomatoes*
- *Lebanese cucumbers, cut into strips*
- *Peas in the pod*
- *Strips of yellow, red or green capsicum*
- *Whole green beans*

Dairy

You read everywhere that experts suggest you include one serve of dairy food in a lunch box every day. One serve is equal to:

- *250ml of milk. In the summer, try freezing milk overnight and wrap in a cloth for the lunch box to minimize the sweating - by lunchtime it will be ready to drink.*
- *Cheese slices, cubes or sticks*
- *Yoghurt - natural or fruit yoghurt. Try freezing a tub of yoghurt and placing in the lunch box. As with the milk – by lunchtime, it will have partially thawed and be ready to eat.*

Protein food

Choose one or more of these protein rich foods as a starter for your sandwich:

- *Baked beans (choose low salt where available; consider trying Mexican, barbeque, curried flavours)*
- *Bean salad*
- *3 bean mix*
- *Canned fish, such as sardines, mackerel*
- *Cheese*
- *Egg (hard boiled, lightly curried)*
- *Falafel*
- *Fish patties*
- *Lentil patties*
- *Peanut butter*
- *Plain unsalted nuts (1/3 cup)*
- *Sliced cold meats such as ham, turkey, smoked salmon, chicken, lamb, corned beef, roast beef, ham, cold sliced meatloaf or meatballs*
- *Tuna in brine or salmon. Try the mini cans of tuna with added flavours, such as tuna and sun-dried tomatoes, or tuna and lemon.*

Sandwiches

Try to include lots of varieties of bread, fillings and spreads, to retain interest in sandwiches.   Breads/rolls; wholemeal, multigrain, rye, corn, flat, pita, sourdough, pumpernickel, mountain, lavash, white fibre-enriched, omega 3 enriched, soy and linseed, herb ... The list goes on.

- *Bagels*
- *Corn thins*
- *Crackers*
- *Crispbreads*
- *Crumpets*
- *English muffins*
- *Foccacias*
- *Fruit loaf/buns*
- *Mountain bread - try wheat, corn, rice or barley*
- *Pasta and rice: make a salad with Italian dressing, chunks of cheese and lots of raw vegetables*
- *Pikelets*
- *Pita pocket bread*
- *Rice: try our easy fried rice recipe and add lots of steamed vegetables*
- *Rice cakes*
- *Scones*

Super Sandwich Ideas

Gathered from some Super Mummies in our lives!

1. Roast beef, tomato, grainy mustard and shredded iceberg lettuce
2. Peanut butter and mashed banana
3. Cheese, vegemite and a sprinkling of finely chopped onion
4. Peanut butter and bean sprouts (sounds unusual but is really tasty!!)
5. Banana on raisin bread
6. Cheese with grated carrot, lettuce and sultanas
7. Tuna and tomato
8. Baked beans on a bread roll
9. Chicken, chopped celery and walnuts and a dash of mayo. to combine
10. Cottage cheese mixed with chopped apple and dates (yummo!)
11. Ham, chutney, lettuce and grated carrot and cheese on a foccacia
12. Egg and lettuce
13. Apple and cream cheese
14. Salmon mixed with cream cheese to bind
15. Cheese and tomato
16. Ham and cheese
17. Cream cheese, chopped celery and sultanas
18. Peanut butter and grated carrot
19. Leftover roast meat with grated carrot, chopped lettuce and chutney
20. Tuna, lettuce and tomato sauce
21. Ham, cheese and a pineapple ring (make sure it is dry before placing on the sandwich)
22. Mashed banana
23. Grated carrot, cheese and mayonnaise
24. Curried egg
25. Bacon, lettuce and tomato.

A More Exciting Sandwich

1. *Triple Deckers – this is really easy and fun.*
    Make a sandwich with   3 slices of bread and two layers
    of filling. Remove the crusts and cut into three strips.

2. *Pita Pockets – half a pocket bread filled with your choice*
    of filling, e.g. lean meat, salad, egg, grated cheese, carrot, etc.

3. *As above, use a variety of different breads.*

4. *Pack sandwich fillings separately so that children can make*
    their own sandwiches to avoid, "They're too soggy!!"

5. *Buy different cutting shapes for your toddlers (use the excess*
    for breadcrumbs to avoid waste) but it is fun for them to
    eat a shark-shaped sandwich!!

Nut Butter Sandwiches

Makes 1

- *1 cup of chopped nuts (choose from cashews, almonds, macadamia, walnuts or peanuts)*
- *2 tbs. sultanas (or raisins)*
- *1 tsp. macadamia nut oil (or extra virgin olive oil)*
- *2 slices wholemeal bread, per person*

Blend the nuts and sultanas together in a food processor to make a smooth, thick paste (this takes some time). Add the oil to get the right consistency for your spread. Spread one side of the bread with the nut butter and place the other slice of bread over the top and cut into four. Serve. Extra nut spread can be kept in the fridge for up to one week in a sealed jar.

Dried Fruit - Banana Chips

- *4 bananas*

Peel and slice banana thinly. Bake in a hot oven 220C for 15-20 minutes, or until crisp.

Others

You can purchase a really wide variety of dried fruits from supermarkets and health food stores.

Or, if you are like, Errol McCosker (Kim's Dad), dry them with your own dehydrator ... his dried mango is simply divine and his grandchildren love it!

Food Safety and Hygiene Tips for Lunch boxes

1. Use an insulated lunch box or carry bag
2. Use a frozen ice brick or drink bottle in the lunch box
3. Freeze sandwiches the night before as both a time saver and to keep foods cool
4. Chill cooked foods, e.g. boiled egg, before packing in the lunch box
5. Store lunchbox in a cool spot
6. Wash little (and big) hands thoroughly before eating, and after going to the toilet or playing with pets
7. Wash lunch box thoroughly after school every day.

Saving for your Child's Education

By Kim McCosker

As a financial planner for the past several years, I find that a frequent concern for most parents is saving for their children's education. With average private school fees nearing $10,000 per annum and 2 or more children often at school at the same time, this is a lot of net dollars to come up with at some point in the future.

How do you do that?

Like most forms of saving, the earlier you start the better - particularly if you are hoping to send your child to a private school at some point. There are two reasons for starting to save early:

1.   You will receive the benefit of compounding interest on your savings (you earn interest on interest)

2.   You can afford to take a longer-term view and can invest in "growth" assets - such as shares - instead of putting your money into a bank account, a "defensive" asset.

Because penalty tax rates apply to children's income that they didn't work for, such as investment income, most people prefer to save in their own name and set aside the money for the child's education. If you or your partner is on a lower tax rate, consideration should be given to investing the savings in that person's name, rather than incurring tax on a higher-than-needed marginal rate.
See the following for 2006/07 tax rates:

2006/07 thresholds	Marginal tax rate	Tax payable (Resident)
< $6,000	Nil	Nil
$6,001 - $25,000	15%	Nil + 15% of excess over $6,000
$25,001 - $75,000	30%	2,850 + 30% of excess over $25,000
$75,001 - $150,000	40%	17,850 + 40% of excess over $75,000
>$150,000	45%	14,850 + 45% of excess over $150,000

Whilst there are a lot of different investment options available, financial advisers often recommend managed funds as good vehicles to save for a child's education, as you can choose an investment strategy that suits you with the money being professionally managed.

Usually you need to invest a minimum amount of $1,000 to buy into a managed fund, although some let you start your investment with as little as $500; however they require you to commit to a regular savings plan where you add to your investment on a monthly basis from as little as $100.   Note; often when the account balance exceeds a certain limit you are able to suspend this payment.

Essentially, when you invest in a managed fund, you are buying units of equal value in the fund. For example, if you invest $500 in the '4 Ingredient Fund' today and its unit price is $1, you will buy 500 units. If the value of the underlying investments owned by the fund rises, then so too does the value of your units, e.g. If your unit price increases to $1.02, your account balance will increase to $510 ($1.02 x 500).

Conversely, if the value of the underlying investments fall, then, so too, does the value of your units, e.g. If your unit price decreases to $0.98, your account balance will decrease to $490 ($0.98 x 500).

What is really important here is to know and understand what the underlying assets of your chosen fund are and who is managing them. When you know and understand this, rather than panic on a day when your unit price is down you may even begin thinking that this represents a good buying opportunity – a bargain (don't you just love those words!).

What if you don't have the minimum investment for a managed fund?

It makes sense to build up your savings in a high-interest bank account until you have enough funds to invest in a higher earning product. Ask your bank, as most have online or bonus saver style accounts that pay higher rates of interest. Most banking institutions offer these now and if they don't, find one that does and remember to check the fine print for any special conditions.

Where do you start?

If you have the funds you need, contact the Financial Institution you select and complete a Product Disclosure Statement (PDS).

If you are still confused, or would like to confirm a question or two, simply email; info@4ingredients.com.au.

When do you start??   NOW!!

Disclaimer: This information has been provided as general advice only.
4 Ingredients strongly recommends that you seek specific advice prior
to making any kind of investment.

A recipe
for all Mothers

Today I left some dishes dirty;
The bed I made at 3:30
The nappies soaked a little longer,
The odour grew a little stronger.
The crumbs I spilt the day before
Are staring at me from the floor.
The fingerprints, there on the wall
Will likely still be there, next fall.
The dirty streaks on the window panes
Will still be there next time it rains.
"Shame on you old lazy-bones," I say
"And just what have you done, today?"

I nursed a baby till he slept,
I held a toddler while he wept.
I played a game of hide and seek
I squeezed a toy, so it would squeak.
I pulled a wagon, sang a song,
Taught a child right from wrong.
What did I do this whole day through?
Not much that shows, I guess it's true...
Unless you think that what I've done
Might be important to someone
With bright blue eyes and soft blonde hair
If that is true, I've done my share.

Joanne Green

Drinks

"BE FABULOUS!" love Kim & Rach

Apple, Carrot & Ginger Juice

A great breakfast drink!

- *2 granny smith apples*
- *2 carrots*
- *1 tbs. fresh ginger*

Blend or juice; don't peel, as most of the vitamins are found just beneath the skin.

Apple, Celery & Carrot Juice

- *2 granny smith apples*
- *2 celery sticks (it's best to remove the strings)*
- *2 carrots*

Blend or juice.

Banana & Maple Supreme

- *½ cup chilled milk*
- *1 ripe banana*
- *2 tsp. maple syrup*

Blend altogether. Pour into a large glass and decorate with a slice of banana.

Energiser Drink

- *1 ripe banana*
- *½ cup fresh or frozen berries (strawberries or raspberries or mixed berries)*
- *½ cup skim milk*
- *¼ cup low-fat natural yoghurt*

Combine all ingredients in a blender and blend until smooth. Add ½ cup of ice for frappe effect. Serve in a tall glass.

Fresh Lemonade

- *8 lemons, juiced and pulped*
- *1 cup fructose*
- *1 .5 cups ice cubes*
- *2.5 cups sparkling or still, filtered water.*

Put the lemon juice, fructose and ice cubes in a blender to liquidize and to break up the ice and melt the fructose. Add water slowly and mix well. Serve.

Grape Melon Drink

- *¼ watermelon*
- *1 bunch of grapes, without stalk*

Blend or juice.

Melon Delight

- *¾ cup pineapple juice*
- *4 slices honeydew melon*
- *1 tsp. honey*

Blend the ingredients with ½ a cup of ice and pour into a large glass.

Orange, Lemon & Strawberry Juice

- *2 oranges*
- *1 lemon*
- *1 cup strawberries*

Peel oranges and lemon and quarter, add strawberries and blend. This is a great 'fresh start' juice.

Orange & Yoghurt Shake

- *2 large oranges*
- *1 cup of natural Greek yoghurt*
- *1 tsp. honey*

Peel oranges and place in a blender with yoghurt and honey.

Peanut, Pine & Banana Shake

- *500g organic yoghurt*
- *2 chilled bananas*
- *2 cups chilled organic pineapple pieces, or fresh pineapple*
- *½ cup smooth organic peanut butter*

Combine all ingredients in a blender and process till smooth.

Pina Colada Shake

Recipe from Cyndi O'Meara.

- *1 pineapple, juiced*
- *1 cup coconut milk*
- *2 bananas*
- *1 cup ice*

Combine all ingredients in a blender and process till smooth. Serve chilled.

Pineapple & Mint Juice

- *1 pineapple*
- *5 sprigs fresh mint leaves*

Blend well and serve chilled.

Strawberry Smoothie

- *1 cup chilled organic apple juice*
  (if more than 90% juice, or 4 apples)
- *2 ripe bananas*
- *1 tbs. flaxseed oil*
- *1 punnet chilled strawberries, washed and hulled*

Blend all ingredients together and serve chilled. YUM!

Great Combination Meals

As suggested by a Chef with over 20 years experience.

Beef

1. Beef Wellington, beef stock & red wine reduction, beans, garlic and pine nuts
2. Pesto stuffed steak, mushroom risotto, rocket, oven-roasted tomato
3. Quick meatloaf, mixed green salad, balsamic and garlic dressing
4. Roast Beef, seasoned roast vegetables, best ever gravy, damper

Chicken

1. Chicken, pumpkin and chickpea curry, fluffy rice, yoghurt and pappadams
2. Cheese and prosciutto chicken, sweet potato and baby spinach
3. Cajun chicken kebab, spinach and strawberry salad, chilli mayonnaise
4. Mascarpone and coriander chicken, garlic potato and green salad with balsamic and garlic dressing.

Fish

1. Baked salmon with pesto crust, polenta, English spinach, shaved parmesan & marinated olives
2. Herb baked barramundi, sautéed lemon potato, asparagus & balsamic dressing
3. Moroccan salmon, antipasto tart, hummus, rocket lettuce
4. Pasta with crab and lemon cream, green salad, vinaigrette, garlic bread

Lamb

1. Lamb shank casserole, mash potato with pine nuts, seasoned roast vegetables
2. Asian lamb cutlets, onion jam, Queensland beer battered vegetables, coriander
3. Tandoori lamb cutlets, Greek yoghurt and egg mayonnaise, avocado salsa
4. Lamb and bacon parcels, spring salad, balsamic and garlic dressing

Pork

1. Chinese BBQ pork, soba noodles & easy Thai dressing
2. Pork & bacon wrap, brie bruschetta, olive oil, fresh basil
3. Pork tenderloin with mustard sauce, rosemary and thyme potato, asparagus butter & parmesan
4. Roast pork, grilled pears, roasted corn with parmesan & cayenne, best ever gravy

Vegetarian

1. *Sour cream quiche, green salad with Greek yoghurt and egg mayonnaise dressing*
2. *Green bean curry, fluffy rice, yoghurt, pappadams*
3. *Pasta with tomato and basil, brie bruschetta (with or without tomatoes)*
4. *Mushroom risotto, shaved parmesan, roasted tomato, rocket and asparagus.*

Notes

Handy Home Tips

Interesting Tips for the Household

This book has 'morphed' into what it has ultimately become. When you start to tell people what you are working on they come up with some fabulous suggestions. One such suggestion was to include a 'Handy Home Tips' section.

Here follows some of those terrific little tips, gathered from some of our nearest and dearest.

Alleviate discomfort when plucking your eyebrows: By smoothing baby teething gel over the area to numb the pain.

Bandaids: Removing is easy if you soak a piece of cotton wool in baby oil and rub over the tape.

Blender: Cleaning your blender is much quicker if you fill it about a third with hot water and add a couple of drops of your washing detergent, then turn it on!

Boiling Pasta: Add at least 4-5 cups of water to a large pot. One tablespoon of salt should be added to the water as it begins to boil. If the salt is added too soon it can give off an odour, which can affect the taste of the pasta. If it is added immediately before the pasta, the salt may not have enough time to completely dissolve in the water. The salt helps bring out the flavour in the pasta and helps it hold its shape.

Brittle & flaking fingernails: Mix 2 level teaspoons of gelatine into 1/2 glass of fruit juice or cold water. Drink at once and repeat daily for at least 6 weeks. You should see a dramatic improvement in your nails after about 2 months.

Brittle nails: To avoid, massage cod liver oil, which is rich in vitamin A, into cuticles and nails. After three months, nails will be stronger and cuticles smoother.

Broken Glass: Use a piece of bread to pick up the fragments of broken glass.

Brunette or red hair: To add shine, after shampooing rinse with fresh brewed black coffee which you have cooled, followed by cold water.

Carry a water bottle with you at all times: Water flushes toxins in the body, as well as filling you up.

Celery: Stop celery wilting by wrapping it in alfoil, when putting in the refrigerator, and it will keep for weeks.

Chewing gum in children's hair: Dab with a cloth soaked with eucalyptus oil, gum should come out without tears.

Cockroaches: To repel, mix equal parts of borax and sugar and place where cockroaches frequent, e.g. under fridge and dishwashers.

Disinfectant: Teatree oil, added to cleaners or in the rinsing water, is a natural disinfectant.

Drains of your sink: To clean, put a tbs. of bicarbonate of soda down the sink followed by two tbs. of vinegar, and let stand.

Eyes: Relax your eyes at regular intervals when reading or using a computer by taking regular 5 minute breaks, or focusing at a distance of 5 metres away.

Fabric interior of your car: To remove marks from, use home brand baby wipes; even the long-term stains will come off ... these really do work!

Fish: To cook fish, it generally takes 10 minutes to cook, per inch of thickness. Just to be sure it doesn't overcook, start checking the fish at 7-8 minutes.

Flowers: Cutting an inch off the bottom of the stems and placing into water within 13 seconds (prevents inhalation of air) and adding a little bleach in the water will keep your flowers longer, because the water is cleaner. Change water regularly.

Fridges and freezers: To keep smelling fresh, sprinkle a few drops of vanilla essence onto a damp cloth and wipe the interior walls and shelves. To dispel odours, place a small container of bicarbonate of soda inside the fridge.

For an instant facelift: Beat an eggwhite and apply it to your skin. Leave on for about 10 minutes and rinse off. Your skin will be tighter and appear firmer.

For puffy eyes: Soak two tea bags, then place them in the freezer for a few minutes; place on eyes & lay back & relax! Or, grate a raw potato, mould it into a mushy pack, and put it on your eyes and lids for 10-20 minutes. The potato starch will help smooth eye-area skin and ease away puffiness.

Green hair: Remove the green tinge from your hair, as a result of swimming in chlorinated water, by washing your hair in 5 aspirin tablets dissolved in a third cup of shampoo. Or alternatively, 3 tbs. of vinegar in your shampoo.

Housework: Hire help, or barter for help. If you can't afford a weekly cleaner, employ someone to do the hard work once a fortnight – work this into your budget; it is worth every cent of the exhilarating feeling that walking into a clean house offers!!

Iceberg lettuce: Lasts much longer if wrapped in alfoil before placing it in the vegetable tray in the fridge. And it's especially good during winter when you don't use lettuce much.

Iron: To clean the underneath, wipe it with a cloth soaked in cold tea. This will remove stains immediately.

Leather lounge suite: To clean, wash it with warm, soapy water using a nail brush and cloth. Allow to dry then smother the cleaned area with Vaseline; rub it in with a cloth to get the residue off. This works better than most expensive cleaners.

Leather Lounge: To revive, polish it with linseed oil and vinegar, in portions of 1:2.

Lower back pain: To relieve, sleep with a pillow under your knees to take the pressure off your lower back and have a good nights sleep.

Make-do hair spray: Getting ready for a big night out and realise you're out of hair spray? Try dissolving a tablespoon of sugar in a glass of hot water, wait till it cools and then put into a spray bottle. It's effective and environmentally friendly, too!

Mascara : As it gets older and starts to dry up, soak in a mug of hot water before use.

Meat: Remove from fridge about an hour before BBQ'ing. Your meat will be more succulent as a result.

Minimise redness of spots on your face: By soaking a piece of cotton wool in eye drops and holding on spot for 20 seconds.

Moths: Repel pantry moths by keeping an open packet of epsom salts on the shelf.

Nail polish: Will last longer if you keep it in the fridge.

Nice smelling car: Place a tube of fabric softener concentrate under the seats (do not pierce; apple and lavender particularly nice). The diversity and staying power of the scents are great and they work better than expensive car deodorisers.

Nicotine stains on fingers: Can be removed by rubbing with nail polish remover or by simply giving up smoking!!

Oven: Reduce the unpleasant smell left from oven cleaners by baking some citrus peelings on a low heat.

Oven Cleaning: To reduce, line the bottom of your oven with aluminium foil cut to size. The foil catches drips and grease, and can be easily replaced when dirty.

Pearls: To clean your pearls, shake in a bag of uncooked rice.

Razor burn: Avoid razor burn after shaving your legs by moisturising beforehand. While shaving cream is the most popular method, try prepping your leg with hair conditioner for a few minutes before shaving. It will hold moisture on the leg longer and provide a very smooth shave.

Remove baked-on stains from glass baking dishes: By soaking in a strong solution of borax and water.

Removing mascara: A cheaper and just as effective way to do this is to use baby oil. Simply dip a cotton bud in, or cover some cotton wool with, baby oil and gently wipe over your lashes. The oil will also soften the skin around your eyes, so there is no need for eye creams, either.

Revitalising eye gel: Keep your eye gel in the fridge to really soothe tired eyes or cool you down on a hot day.

School lunches: Make more fun by using a cooking cutter to cut sandwiches into shapes!

Self-raising flour: To make, mix 2 kg plain flour, 2 tbs. bicarbonate of soda and ¼ cup cream of tartar. Sift well.

Sharp lip-line and eye-line: Put your eye-liner or lip-liner pencil in the freezer, briefly, before sharpening, to get a fine point.

Spaghetti: When cooking, add a tsp. of cooking oil or a tsp. of butter to the water in rice, noodles or spaghetti. This will prevent the water from boiling over and strands from sticking together.

Stainless steel sink: To brighten, use a damp cloth soaked in vinegar.

Steak:

Cook steak in a pan as follows:

1. Oil the steaks, not the pan, using extra virgin olive oil.
2. Set heat on medium.
   Always have the pan hot before starting.
3. Place steaks in pan; do not turn until sealed and
   juices have risen (usually 1 to 1 ½ minutes).
   Turn and continue to cook to desired state.

Cooking Times (depending on thickness):

Rare:	2-5 minutes
Medium:	8-12 minutes
Well:	12-15 minutes

Strawberries: Purchase strawberries red all-over. The redder near the hull of the fruit the sweeter.

Stuck-on food in pots, pans, and casserole dishes: Fill the pan with water and place a fabric softener sheet in the water. Allow the pan to soak overnight. The food will
wipe right out!

Swollen hands: If you have a ring stuck on your finger, due to your fingers swelling, soak your hand in ice water till the ring slips off.

Take the generic brand on prescriptions: They often come from the same company and are exactly the same as the full-priced version.

Tie a small bell to any door: leading out of the house and you'll be able to hear a small child making their escape!

Timber floors: which have been sealed can be cleaned with cold tea on a mop. A little vinegar in the bucket of water with the detergent helps to remove any grease from kitchen floors.

Try using some cold cucumber slices: ... on your eyes at the end of the night to relieve tired eyes. An oldie, but a goodie.

Washing Clothes: Hang clothes as soon as you can after washing, to reduce creasing.

When giving distasteful medicine to young children: First, run an ice cube over their tongue; this temporarily freezes the taste buds.

When starting a new fitness regime: Don't over commit yourself, as you will soon lose interest; start with a little activity and increase as your fitness level does.

When travelling with a baby: Take some bicarbonate of soda with you in a small zip-lock bag. Should your baby be sick, simply sprinkle clothes with the soda. Brush off when dry and odour will have disappeared.

Whiten your fingernail tips: ... by soaking your nails in lemon juice.

Biographies

Rachael Bermingham

Rachael Bermingham was born in Stanthorpe before moving to Australia's Sunshine Coast with her family while still in Primary School. Today she still happily resides there in Mooloolaba with her fabulous husband Paul and gorgeous son Jaxson.

In addition to being the proud co-author of '4 Ingredients', Rachael is a popular and inspiring presenter and speaker and is the owner and co director for many businesses including;

- *www.MarketingToSuccess.com a consultancy firm that guides women on how to build businesses from home.*
- *'LIPS' aka www.LadiesInitiatingProsperityandSuccess.com a seminar and networking group that fast forwards women in achieving their personal and professional goals.*
- *www.SunshineCoastSpeakers.com which is a booking bureau for motivational, educational and informative keynote speakers, entertainers and MC's who reside on the Sunshine Coast.*

All started and developed from a $0 capital using her natural flair and basic business and marketing strategies.

Renowned for her passion, contagious enthusiasm, inspiring resilience and focus, she is a natural entrepreneur selling her first business venture for a profit at just 19 years of age. Her insightfulness and commitment continue to inspire and motivate others to achieve their dreams.

Rachael's lifelong mission is to help as many people as possible to create incomes in a flexible and passive way, so that families and friends can spend more quality time together and thereby build stronger, happier, healthier, and wealthier and more fulfilled communities. This mission drives her to not just walk her talk, but to spread the word by speaking to various social and business groups and organizations to help ignite their imagination and spark ideas of their own personal and professional vision and missions via a variety of topics such as;

- *How to build a profitable business from home.*
- *Know what you want and how to get it.*
- *How to transform your goals into achievements.*
- *Setting yourself up for success.*
- *Life planning for YOUR success.*
- *Understand and use your natural toolbox to steer you to YOUR destiny.*
- *Dreaming, Believing, Creating and Succeeding.*
- *Attitude - the awful and awesome and how it affects your life.*
- *How to get motivated.*
- *How to balance life so you can fit everything in - even time for you!*
- *Overcome challenges and Succeed.*
- *The power of publicity.*
- *How to develop your businesses personality.*
- *Marketing to success from a ZERO budget.*
- *How to discover your passions, hidden talents and skills and profit from them.*
- *Selecting, knowing and attracting your ideal client.*
- *Consciously creating the life you want.*

Rachael is living proof that when you implement ordinary steps you can achieve extraordinary outcomes. In just 18 months she has given birth to gorgeous son Jaxson, developed 3 income producing businesses all run from her home, she has co written 2 books, spoken at multiple seminars, events and conferences and does it all in and around son Jaxson's sleep times so that she can continue to be the full time hands on mum she's always desired to be.

She is featured weekly on talkback radio, has contributed, been quoted and interviewed for a host of newspapers, magazines and TV programs.

With her naturally strategic character, pioneering spirit and enjoyment for helping others live their dreams, Rachael's go getting attitude has been influential in carving out a very exciting and fulfilling career utilizing the strategies and actions she advocates.

You can contact Rachael through the 4 Ingredients website www.4Ingredients.com.au or by mailing to PO Box 1171 Mooloolaba QLD 4557.

Kim McCosker

Kim was born in Stanthorpe and raised there until moving to Mundubbera, Queensland a fantastic little town where many of her wonderful family and friends still live.

Schooled on the Gold Coast, Kim attended Star of the Sea Catholic High School and Griffith University, completing a degree in International Finance in 1998. Kim trained with MLC as a Financial Planner completing her Diploma in Financial Planning through Deakin University in 2000. Kim's natural ease with people, her ability to communicate effortlessly and her cool, country confidence served her extremely well as a successful financial adviser and later as the Queensland State Manager of MLC Private Client Services. Kim worked for 7 years in the finance industry before finally resigning to spend the time raising her beautiful boys. Kim currently contracts from home Paraplanning (someone who writes Financial plans) to a dynamic Brisbane based financial planning company. In addition to this, over the past 7 years, Glen and Kim have bought and renovated several properties, including the 1957 Anglican Church they currently live in. They own 'relic' a second-hand store in Brisbane's West End and co-own a fabulous Café in Mundubbera called Bella Boo. Kim maintains the administration, bookwork and finances for their various businesses and financial interests.

Without a sliver of doubt however, the most rewarding of everything accomplished to date has been the birth of her two precious little boys Morgan 4 and Hamilton 18 months. To spend more time kicking a footy with them in the yard rather than toiling in the kitchen, the idea of quick, easy and delicious meal planning was born from necessity rather than Kim's kitchen know-how! And this is where we are today, co-author of "4 Ingredients" a cookbook Kim hopes helps busy people everywhere to create simple yet savoury food without breaking the budget and relieving them of unnecessary time in the kitchen!

You can contact Kim through the 4 Ingredients website www.4Ingredients.com.au or by emailing her at info@4ingredients. com.au or by telephoning (0430) 178 781.

Bibliography

Books

Cyndi O'Meara. Changing Habits Changing Lives. Penguin Books Victoria Australia 2000.

Cyndi O'Meara. Changing Habits Changing Lives Cookbook. Penguin Books Victoria Australia 2002.

Donalee Halkett. Snack it Out. Choice Living Po Box 1546, Noosa Heads Queensland Australia 4567.

The Australian Womens Weekly Cookbooks. Great Vegetarian Food. Sydney, Australia. ACP Publishing Pty Ltd, 2001.

Family Circle. Kids Party Book. Sydney, Australia. Murdoch Magazines Pty Ltd, 1995.

Lowery, Barbara. Quick & Easy Cookbook. 176 South Creek Road, Dee Why West, Australia. Summit Books, 1977.

Slater, Nigel. The 30-Minute Cook. 27 Wrights Lane, London W8 5TZ, Great Britain. Penguin Group, 1994.

Bjelke- Petersen, Lady Flo. Classic Country Collection. Sydney, Australia. New Holland Publishers, Pty Ltd, 1997.

Concept New Zealand & R & R Kitchens. Fast Meals. PO Box 254 Carlton North, Victoria, Australia. R & R Publications Marketing Pty Ltd, 2005.

Burt, Alison. Fondue Cookery. 176 South Creek Road, Dee Why West, Australia. Summit Books, 1970.

Lloyd Susan. Dinner Party Cookbook. 169 Phillip Street, Waterloo, N.S.W. Australia. Australian Universities Press Pty Ltd, 1974.

Cooking up a storm from the IGA Cauldren Pot. Mundubbera IGA. Self-published, 2004.

Crofts, Susan. Susan's Kitchen. Mundubbera, Queensland. Self published, 2005.

Webpage

"Chefs Feed Your Passion." 23 December, 2005. www.chefs.com/recipes

Sydney Markets. "Healthy Recipes." www.betterhealth.vic.gov.au

"Parentbytes Recipes." Edition 49. www.parentbytes.com

Krosch, Renee. "The Easiest and Tastiest Chicken Recipes Around." ABC Victoria.

8 May 2006. www.abc.net.au

Annabella's Kitchen. " Lamb, Beef & Pork Recipes." www.annabella.net

Larsen, Linda. "Busy Cooks Recipe Box" 21 June 2006. www.busycooks.about.com

Asoliva. "Spain." www.globalgourmet.com

An Australian Government, State and Territory health initiative. "Why 2 & 5."

http://www.gofor2and5.com.au/

"Easy Meals to Cook" May 2006. http://www.xpress101meal.com/

Index of Contents

4 Ingredients

4 Ingredients

4 Ingredients

4

Ingredients